東京都練馬区石神井町二ノ二一ノ四
長田和香子
北海道砂川市
有)村中商事
北光貸衣裳
村中光子・雄司
平垣和廣
群馬県高崎市
山崎學
サンピエール病院
伸子
平成十九年五月吉日建之
平成二十四年十二月吉日建之
平成十八年三月吉日建之
平成十八年十一月吉日建之

Japan

100 Legendary Places

ROUGH GUIDES

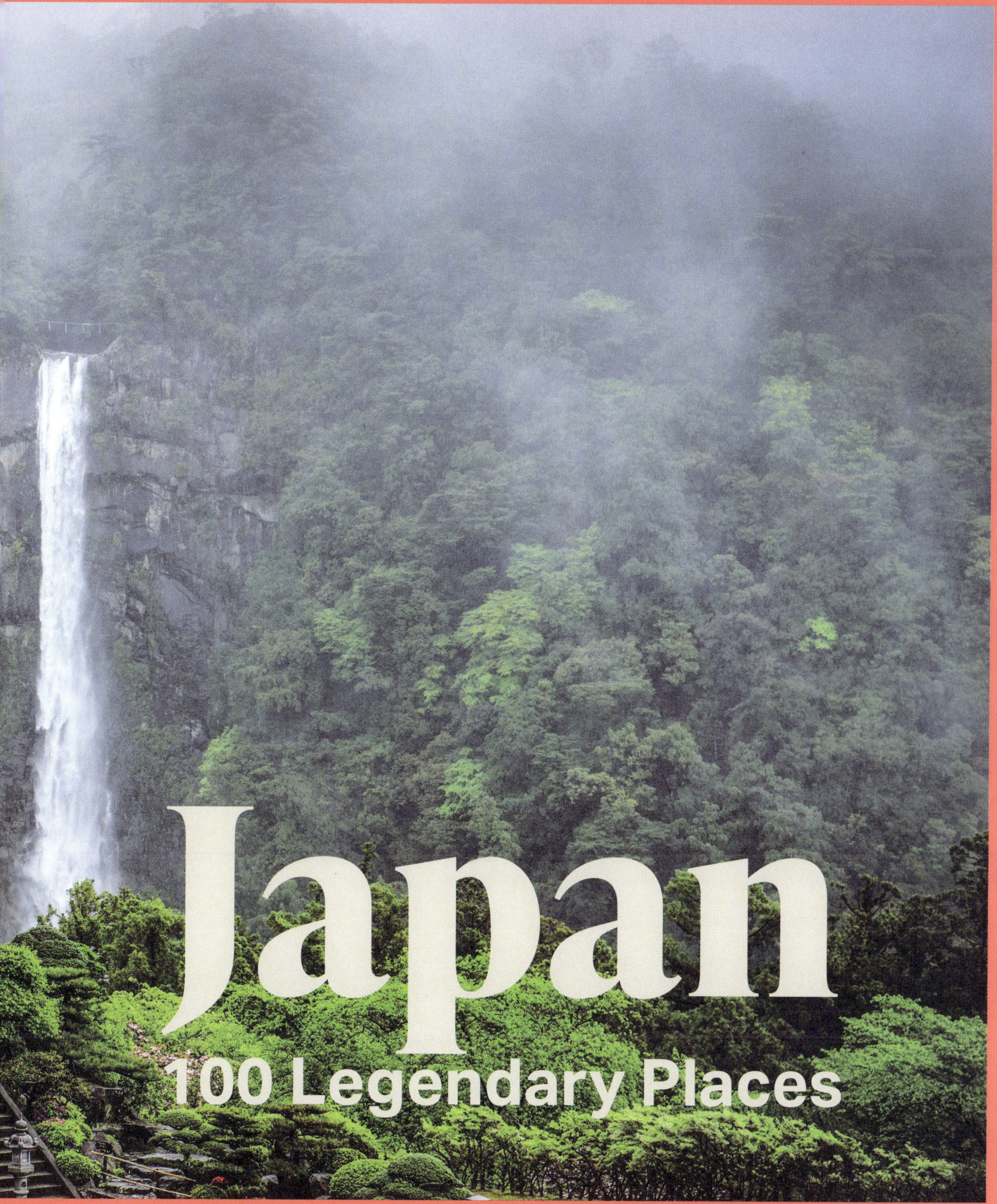

Japan

100 Legendary Places

Japan
100 Legendary Places

Introduction

Japan is at its most addictive when you stop trying to pin it down and let it lead. Tokyo dazzles – all sushi and sumo, neon and noodles – piling up into a glorious sensory overload. Yet the real magic often comes when you drift off course and find yourself in a tiny six-stool bar, watching temple smoke curling above backstreets, or stumbling upon a neighbourhood festival by chance.

Beyond the big names, Japan makes a habit of shifting under your feet. Its ancient capitals trade in refinement and ritual, while port cities and mountain towns tell a more everyday version of the country's story. Volcanic landscapes steam and hiss, cedar forests swallow old paths and the sea breaks the map into islands that range from the world-famous to the almost-forgotten. Far to the north, wide skies and wild parks reveal Japan at its most rugged, while in the south, the Ryūkyū chain brings turquoise seas, coral reefs, subtropical colour and nights made for stargazing.

These are not simply the greatest hits or a bucket list to tick off. Our 100 legendary places offer scenes that lodge in the memory – icons that live up to the hype, alongside the detours, oddities and once-in-a-lifetime moments that turn a trip into a tale you'll keep retelling.

Hokkaidō

An unspoiled frontier, Hokkaidō feels like the country's wild north – romanticized perhaps, yet genuinely untamed. Forests roll to the horizon, and its vast national parks are home to roaming wildlife, snowy slopes, restless volcanoes and bubbling onsen. Yet stylish Sapporo and historic Hakodate mean you're never far from the comforts of city life. With the bullet train whisking you there, there's little excuse not to fall under its northern spell.

らあめん
ひぐま
KUNI
MITSU
麺
SAPPORO

Sapporo

Sapporo operates as Hokkaidō's hinge – a place many plan to pass through, as a major transport hub – but then end up lingering in. More than just a gateway, and home to nearly two million people and an easy-to-navigate grid plan, the city of Sapporo is generously endowed with parks and gardens. The mountains that attract skiers and snowboarders rise up to its south, and the dramatic coastline around the Shakotan Peninsula is less than thirty minutes away. After dark, lively Susukino really sparks into life – a neon-bright sprawl of bars, restaurants and clubs where ramen alleys do a brisk late trade and the nightlife feels as full-throttle as anywhere outside Tokyo or Osaka. Indeed, beer is the city's other calling card. The Sapporo Beer Museum and Beer Garden occupy a handsome red-brick complex, combining brewing history with the simple pleasure of settling in for a glass and a plate of *jingisukan* lamb. In summer, outdoor beer gardens make the most of Ōdōri Park, the broad green strip running through the city centre.

(L) Nightlife on a Sapporo bar street; (T) Hill of the Buddha, Makomanai Takino Cemetery; (B) Braving snowy streets in winter

Niseko

Niseko has become Japan's winter sports headline act for good reason: impressive amounts of perfect powder snow and top-class, interlinked ski fields, with scenery anchored by the near-perfect cone of Mount Yōtei, the local "Ezo Fuji". The main village, Hirafu, has absorbed most of the development, much of it via foreign investment, which helps explain the unusually international feel once the season kicks in. In winter, it's all ski lifts, backcountry adventures and late dinners; outside ski season, the same landscape turns into an adventure playground for rafting, mountain biking, kayaking and hiking, with trails on Yōtei and Annupuri delivering wide-open views. Niseko's secret is that it doesn't rely on snow alone – the place has momentum year-round, and it shows in the quality of the food and accommodation as much as on the slopes.

(L) Surveying Mount Yotei from Takahashi Dairy Farm

Hakodate

Arriving in Hakodate feels like stepping into a different side of Hokkaidō – older, more outward-looking, shaped by its early role as one of Japan's first ports opened to foreign trade after the mid-nineteenth century treaties. Trams rattle you between districts, and the city's best wandering potential is in Motomachi, where steep streets and late nineteenth- and early twentieth-century buildings include churches, consulates and wooden houses, giving things a faintly trans-Pacific air (indeed, it's known as the San Francisco of Japan). Above it all rises Hakodate-yama. In daylight the view is expansive, but at night the panorama is spectacular: a soaring vista of harbour lights, the curve of the port and squid boats glowing offshore. Seafood is part of the draw too, with the atmospheric morning market showcasing the day's catch and the city's long connection to the sea. Come for the history and the hillside streets, then stay out late for the view.

(L) Springtime sakura bloom; (T) Fog over Motomachi, or is it San Francisco?; (B) King crab at Hakodate morning market

Noboribetsu

(T) Noboribetsu's volcanic landscape

Noboribetsu delivers the onsen experience in a strikingly dramatic setting. The landscape is volcanic and sulphurous, with steam and a mineral tang in the air, and the appeal is clear: get up close to the raw geology, with a walk through otherworldly terrain, then retreat into the calm rituals of a traditional *ryokan* and a long soak. It's the contrast between the two that brings the experience to life – the elemental heat outside, the composed comfort within – and it's easy to see why this place has such a reputation for restoration and relaxation. It takes one or two hours to explore the area, wandering along wooden pathways through a landscape of rusty red rocks, streaked green and white by mineral deposits, ending up at Ōyu-numa, a malevolent-looking hot-water lake. Afterwards, you can soothe your feet in a natural footbath. Bring good footwear, as the paths can be slippery.

Daisetsu-zan National Park

Daisetsu-zan is Hokkaidō at its most mountainous: a huge national park stitched with trails, gorges, hot springs and high peaks, including Asahi-dake, the island's tallest. Here, a week can pass without exhausting the possibilities, from a choice of bases. Asahi-dake Onsen stays low-key, a small cluster of lodgings tucked into the forest beneath the ropeway that whisks hikers and skiers up to a landscape of steaming pools and rocky outcrops. Over on the northeast edge, Sōunkyō Onsen is the busier base, but for good reason: the Sōunkyō Gorge, where jagged cliffs rise high above the Ishikari-gawa, and waterfalls such as Ginga and Ryūsei. In summer, the mountain slopes are carpeted with alpine flowers, while September and October bring vivid autumn colours – this is arguably the best season for hiking. In winter, both Asahi-dake and Kuro-dake attract skiers, benefiting from one of the longest ski seasons in Japan.

(O) Cable car over autumnal colours; (L) Flowing waterfall;
(T) Displays at the Sōunkyō Ice Waterfall Festival;
(B) In Sōunkyō's visitor centre

在東海仙薬不老
不死告夢也
卑弥呼なる
神代を想う
濡れ羽根の
海藻干したる
宇賀の浜鳴り
修子
えんがわ
ENGAWA

Otaru

Otaru is small, coastal and atmospheric, a former trading port that wears its past lightly. The canal is the obvious draw, lined with old warehouses that have been repurposed as cafés, shops and galleries, creating a gentle, walkable centre. Look beyond the postcard view, however, and the town's real pleasures lie in the details: narrow streets climbing away from the water, historic buildings tucked between more ordinary houses and the salty maritime air that whets the appetite for seafood. Otaru's craft reputation is equally easy to enjoy at street level, especially in its glass studios and specialist shops, and there's a quiet satisfaction in drifting between them without any need to rush. Otaru's romantic, old-world atmosphere is best appreciated on a slow afternoon and an unhurried evening, enjoying the softening of the lights over the harbour.

(L) Vibrant banners featuring traditional Japanese art hang above storefronts on Sakaimachi-dōri, a preserved merchant street in Otaru

Shiretoko Peninsula National Park

One of Japan's great wild edges, Shiretoko is a UNESCO-listed peninsula pushing into the Sea of Okhotsk, with few roads, scant development and a sense that nature still sets the terms. Wildlife is abundant – deer and foxes are common and brown bears remain a defining presence – and the best months for hiking and exploring the lakes run from early summer into early autumn. The Shiretoko Go-ko (Five Lakes) offer the classic introduction: jewel-like pools of still water linked by raised boardwalks and quiet forest paths, where reflections of spruce and broadleaf trees ripple across the surface. From Utoro, boat trips are the way to experience the harsher coastline, while drift ice litters the shore in winter and some two thousand Steller's sea eagles can be observed near Rausu. Virtually untouched by human development, this is a place that feels genuinely remote, even by Hokkaidō standards.

(O) A male Blakiston's fish owl, the largest species of owl, on Shiretoko; (L) Sunset over the peninsula; (T) There is a large population of Yezo brown bears around Shiretoko

Furano–Biei

Evoking Provençal France, with bales of hay scattered across fields and lone poplars standing against the peaks of Daisetsu-zan National Park, Furano is the Hokkaidō countryside at its most vivid. In summer, the region is known for its colour – rows of lavender and seasonal blooms stretching across the fields around Biei and Bibaushi – but it's not just a pretty landscape. The fertile soil produces a rich range of local produce, from melons and milk to grapes, and that abundance shows up in places like the local winery and cheese factory, where rural production is turned into something you can taste. In winter, the focus shifts to skiing, with the slope-side village atmosphere around Kitanomine making it easy to slide from lifts to dinner without much friction. There is no mistaking the seasons here: Furano's landscape transforms from bright and pastoral in summer to crisp and snow-bound in winter, always rooted in the environment.

(L) Colourful flower fields in summer; (T) Admiring a Furano lavender field; (B) A blanket of snow covers the land in winter

Rishiri-tō & Rebun-tō

Off the northern tip of Hokkaidō, Rishiri-tō and Rebun-tō sit in the Sea of Japan like a final, windswept punctuation mark. Rebun is the gentler of the two, a low-lying island where the big draw is walking coastal paths that, in season, erupts with wild flowers and alpine plants, turning even an easy hike into something quietly memorable. Rishiri is the opposite: a steep-sided volcanic cone rising cleanly from the water, with Rishiri-zan dominating every view and giving the island a more rugged, mountaineering feel. Around both islands, fishing villages and empty stretches of coast keep the pace slow, while local specialities such as *konbu* seaweed and *uni* (sea urchin roe) make meals feel as connected to the place as the landscape. Between them, Rishiri-tō and Rebun-tō represent Hokkaidō at its most remote and restorative, and outside peak season, it's quite possible you'll have much of the islands to yourself.

(O) Momoiwa Hiking Trail, Rebun-tō; (L) Walking trails around the island; (T) RIshiri-zan's imposing cone; (B) Shrine atop Rishiri-zan

Tōhoku

When Matsuo Bashō set out along the "narrow road to the deep north", he felt he was heading for the ends of the earth – and Tōhoku still carries that edge-of-the-map allure. Beyond the cities lies a land where rural rites endure and folklore lingers in misty valleys. Ruined castles and samurai towns guard old secrets, spirits such as *kappa* are said to dwell in rivers while *yamabushi* tread remote peaks, and Osore-zan whispers of purgatory beneath brooding skies.

Sendai

(T) Zuihō-den mausoleum

Known as the "City of Trees", Sendai feels greener and more spacious than many Japanese cities. Broad, tree-lined streets give it an airy feel, and the centre is lively without being relentless, making it a comfortable base for striking out into the rest of Tōhoku. The city's story is inseparable from Date Masamune, the one-eyed warlord who shaped Sendai's rise, and you can still trace his legacy on Aobayama, where the castle once stood above the river and ravines. For a more intimate sense of that history, Zuihō-den, Masamune's richly decorated mausoleum, lies in quiet woodland a short ride from the city centre. Come back down to street level for the city's everyday pleasures, which take in arcades, evening *izakaya*, and a proudly local food culture.

Matsushima Bay

A magnificent watery maze of wooded, temple-topped islands, threaded through with mysterious channels and scattered with secret inlets, Matsushima Bay is officially designated one of Japan's top three scenic areas. The landscape's beauty is made of fragments: hundreds of small islands scattered across the bay, each one topped with wind-shaped pines and edged by pale rock. The best way to appreciate it is to move through it, letting the water and shifting angles do their work. Boats slip out among the islets for the big-picture perspective, but the shoreline delivers its own quieter pleasures, especially once you step beyond the first souvenir strip. Zuigan-ji, approached through a cedar avenue, adds depth with its Date Masamune-era grandeur, while nearby Entsū-in brings calm with its exquisite raked gravel garden and rich clan history. Even the small footbridges out to Godai-dō feel like part of the rhythm, drawing you towards the sea air and back again.

(L) Peaceful paths amidst temples on Godai-dō; (T) Cherry blossoms fringe the coastline; (B) Black-headed gull

Hiraizumi

Hiraizumi is a small town with a magnificent past, a reminder that power once flowed strongly through Japan's north. For a brief period in the twelfth century it rivalled Kyoto, built up by the Fujiwara clan in a vision of earthly paradise, and the surviving sites still carry that ambition. Chūson-ji's Konjiki-dō, the "Golden Hall", is the defining monument: compact, intensely ornate and eye-popping in its use of gold leaf and decoration, with the Fujiwara lords resting within. Mōtsū-ji offers a different kind of beauty, a Heian-period garden arranged around a broad pond, designed for slow strolling and changing views rather than a single dramatic reveal. The progression from a dazzling and intimate site to a spacious and meditative one, with gold, water, trees and silence doing much of the storytelling, is what makes Hiraizumi particularly special.

(L) Chūson-ji in Hiraizumi, an UNESCO World Heritage Site

TŌHOKU

Yamadera

The temple complex of Yamadera is one of Tōhoku's most holy places. Set on a steep, rocky hillside, it was founded in 860 by a Zen priest of the Tendai sect, and reached its peak during the Kamakura period (1185–1333). Today around forty temple buildings still stand scattered among the ancient cedars. The village clings to a steep hillside, with the temple complex of Risshaku-ji scattered above it, reached by a long stone stairway that threads through cedar shade and open rock. Over 1100 steps weave their way up past moss-covered Jizō statues, lanterns and prayer wheels, and squeeze between looming rocks carved with prayers and pitted with caves. At the highest temple, Okuno-in, breathless pilgrims tie prayer papers around a mammoth lantern and light small bunches of incense sticks. The cliffside buildings feel improbably placed, as if the mountain itself has agreed to hold them there. Before you set off back downhill, don't miss the views from the terrace of Godai-dō, perched on the cliff-face just beyond the distinctive red Nōkyō-dō pavilion.

(L) Snow-covered Yamadera; (T) A shrine perched high above the valley; (B) Steps pass shrines on the ascent

Tōno Valley

Set in a bowl of low mountains, the Tōno Valley is famed for its folk tales and storytelling, woven throughout its rural landscape. When folklorist Yanagita Kunio visited in 1909, he found a living world of spirits, rituals and tales told as everyday truth, then published *Tōno Monogatari* the following year, based on 118 stories he heard from local storyteller Kyōseki Sasaki. The small town of Tōno still leans into that legacy, though with a light touch. *Kappa*, the water creatures of local lore, appear on postboxes and signs, and the tourist office even hands out *kappa*-catching "permits", with cucumbers as bait. Beyond town, the valley is made for slow exploration, especially by bike, with small museums, folk villages and traditional L-shaped farmhouses that keep the setting grounded in its present, rural reality. A visit here is slow, peaceful, and somewhat like stepping back in time.

(O) A steam locomotive passes by a field of sunflowers;
(L) Illuminated autumn foliage in Tono;
(T) MIst enveloping the local mountains

Kakunodate

Kakunodate is often described as a "little Kyoto" of the north, but its real charm lies in its quiet, self-contained elegance. The old samurai district is the heart of any visit, with wide streets lined by tall hedges that conceal former residences and, beyond them, the clearly defined merchant quarters. In spring, the town becomes famous for its weeping cherry blossom trees, their branches spilling over walls and waterways and turning an already atmospheric district into something briefly unforgettable. Outside *sakura* season, Kakunodate still holds its appeal. The preserved architecture carries the weight of history, giving the town more substance than prettiness alone, and its compact scale makes it easy to stitch together a satisfying day without rushing. It also stands in gentle contrast to Tōhoku's wilder landscapes, as a place where the region's history feels intimate, orderly and close at hand.

(O) A rickshaw ride past samurai houses; (L) Samurai house framed by blossom; (T) Traditonal dress in a traditional neighbourhood; (B) Interior view from a samurai house

Lake Towada

(T) Ferry on Lake Towada

Japan's third-deepest lake, the steep-sided, crystal-clear Towada-ko fills a 300m-deep volcanic crater in the northern portion of the Towada-Hachimantai National Park. While the lake itself is a major destination, for many visitors the real highlight is the approach, over high passes and through deep wooded valleys, a journey that feels both enclosed and expansive at the same time. The water is famously clear, and the best way to understand the lake's scale is to get out on it, watching the shoreline sweep past in long, quiet curves. Yasumiya, the main settlement, has a shaded lakeside setting that makes it a pleasant base, especially if you arrive late in the day as the crowds thin. Life here moves at a calm pace: a slow walk along the shore, stops at viewpoints and time out on the water. Later, a visit to the famous *Statue of the Maidens* by the Lake is a must. Two identical bronze figures circle each other with hands almost touching, suspended in a moment of near-contact.

Oirase Gorge

Oirase is a river valley that offers a series of small pleasures, one after another, until you realise you've been walking far longer than planned. The classic route follows the Oirase-gawa upstream through a narrow, wooded corridor, where water tumbles among ferns and moss-covered rocks and every bend seems to deliver another ice-white waterfall. Join the path at Ishigedo to pick up the best stretch: a gentle 9km walk that feels immersive without being demanding, though the trail occasionally runs alongside the main road for short sections. The gorge is striking in any season, but especially in autumn, when the deciduous woods flare into colour. The payoff comes at Nenokuchi on the shore of Lake Towada, where the landscape suddenly opens out – a striking contrast to the enclosed valley you've just walked through.

(L) A tumbling stream in Oirase valley in autumn; (T) Picture-perfect waterfalls; (B) Oirase gorge in winter

Sannai-Maruyama

Sannai-Maruyama quietly challenges assumptions about ancient Japan. One of the country's largest and most important Jōmon-period settlement sites, it has a scale and sense of permanence that make it particularly compelling. Rather than a temporary camp, it feels like a place where people built, stored, traded and lived, shaping daily life over centuries. The site is laid out so you can move between excavated areas and reconstructions, tracing that story as you go: from the outlines of pit dwellings to the remains of larger structures that hint at communal life. The museum provides essential context, but it is the open-air site that does the evocative work, inviting you to imagine rhythms of foraging, craft and ritual in this northern landscape, offering a rare glimpse of prehistoric life that sits alongside Tōhoku's temples and scenery. Note that in winter, when the site is covered by snow, it's harder to get a sense of the settlement itself – it still looks magnificent, though.

(O, L, T) Jōmon-era structures at Sannai-Maruyama; (B) Deep snow blankets the ancient dwellings

Dewa-sanzan

Dewa-sanzan is pilgrimage country – three sacred mountains bound together by a tradition that treats movement through landscape as a form of worship. Haguro-san is the most accessible, its long cedar-lined approach building atmosphere with every step and drawing you towards an imposing shrine-temple complex where Shintō and Buddhism have long coexisted. From there, the route continues into wilder terrain. Gassan, the highest peak, offers a very different experience, with high meadows and a sense of openness that can feel surprisingly remote. The final mountain, Yudono, is the most sacred, known for rituals that make the experience feel personal rather than touristic. Dewa-sanzan invites participation in acts of reverence along the way, rather than passive observation, making it an immersive experience. For those with limited time, a shorter route between Haguro-san and the lower slopes of Gassan still brings together cedar forest, shrine architecture and open mountain views.

(L) Dewa shrine; (T) Stairs through the forest; (B) Entering a shrine at Haguro-san

Osore-zan

Osore-zan feels like a place where the ground is still unsettled. The "terrible mountain", where Buddhists believe the spirits of the dead linger on their way to paradise, is a bleak crater lake surrounded by a sulphurous desert where small, weathered statues huddle against the bitter winds. It is a compelling, slightly spine-tingling place – an otherworldly landscape where the boundary between life and death feels unusually thin. Though the temple was founded in the ninth century, Osore-zan was already revered in ancient folk religion as a place where dead souls gather. It's easy to see why: the desolate volcanic terrain, with its yellow- and red-stained soil, multicoloured pools and bubbling, malodorous streams, makes for a scene that is harsh, beautiful and unsettling in equal measure. The temple complex gives structure to a visit, but the mood comes from the setting: barren ridges, a lakeshore that can appear almost luminous in certain light, and small offerings of flowers, coins and incense that bring quiet human presence into an otherwise elemental scene. In summer, the atmosphere shifts again when it becomes a place of pilgrimage and mourning, drawing visitors who treat the mountain as more than scenery. Simple offerings and small stupas of stones along the shoreline reinforce the site's distinctive character, one that resists easy description.

(L) A stone statue of Jizo, protector of travellers, in Osore-zan

Kantō

Kantō is iconic Japan in its full, dazzling sprawl. Tokyo, the planet's largest metropolis, is ordered yet bewildering – frenetic and serene in equal measure, with hidden calm tucked behind its busiest streets. Beyond the capital, it barely takes time to reach Nikkō's mountain-based shrine complex, Kamakura's giant bronze Buddha, snow-capped Mount Fuji and Hakone's hot springs. It's where hyperactivity and hush sit side by side.

Asakusa & THE Sumida Riverfront

Asakusa remains Tokyo's most traditional district, and it still knows how to put on a show. Sensō-ji – the city's most venerable Buddhist temple – draws a continual throng of worshippers and sightseers past stalls peddling trinkets and keepsakes, just as they have done for centuries. Amid the inevitable restaurants and fast-food outlets, old-fashioned craft shops display exquisite hair combs, paper fans and calligraphy-adorned brushes, while the whole area hums with an infectious carnival atmosphere. Then there's the Sumida River, which defines Asakusa almost as much as the temple itself. Cross the water for the soaring Tokyo Skytree and the Philippe Starck-designed Asahi Beer Hall, or take the *suijō basu* (water bus) with its large picture windows. It offers a completely different perspective on the city to the usual vantage point – reason enough to hop aboard.

(L) Sensō-ji in a rare quiet moment

Ueno & Yanesen

Ueno is where Tokyo loosens its tie. The prime draw is Ueno Kōen, a broad, slightly unruly patch of green that transforms into the city's premier cherry-blossom destination in spring, before settling back into a pleasantly walkable retreat around Shinobazu Pond for the rest of the year. The park packs in heavyweight culture – a host of excellent museums, including the Tokyo National Museum – along with a few surviving relics of Kan'ei-ji, once a vast temple complex that dominated this hill-top. From there, venture into Ueno's eastern streets to discover its proletarian, Shitamachi roots. Ameyokochō still feels rough-and-ready, with vendors shouting over stalls selling everything from bulk tea and coffee to jewellery and fresh fish, while *yakitori* bars tuck beneath the railway arches. Continue south into Yanesen, the old-neighbourhood pocket around Yanaka, Nezu and Sendagi, for more of that character, best experienced on foot along its narrow streets and back lanes.

(L) Hanami beneath sakura trees; (T) Paddle boat rides on Shinobazu Pond; (B) The torii tunnel to Hanazono Inari Shrine

Nihonbashi & THE old commercial core

Nihombashi is Tokyo's old commercial core in modern dress – close enough to Ginza to share its gloss, but with a more old-money, merchant-city feel. It is anchored by Mitsukoshi, Tokyo's oldest and most prestigious department store, dating back to 1673: elegant, spacious, and still the place to go for high-quality merchandise. Once the heart of Edo's teeming Shitamachi, Nihombashi grew from a cluster of riverside markets into the city's principal financial district. The warehouses and moneylenders of old have given way to banks, brokers and trading companies, but the mood remains briskly transactional. Linger by the bridge and watch the city stream past with purposeful energy. The real pleasure lies in walking without a fixed destination, letting the streets draw you into neighbouring districts. Tune into the rhythms of everyday life, where lunch queues, streams of commuters and an astonishing variety of shops create the atmosphere of a working district with a distinctive pulse.

(O) Nihonbashi bridge; (L) The commercial core at night; (T) Cat model installation in Ginza Six mall; (B) Taking part in Nihonbashi Nichikyo Festival, a colourful parade in Tokyo that features dance troupes from all over Japan

Ginza–Marunouchi

(T) Dusk over Ginza's streets

Ginza is Tokyo's classic shopping district, polished and grown-up, with a long tradition of department stores and flagship boutiques that still set a certain standard for the city. It's also full of smaller cultural pockets, including galleries and cinemas, meaning the area can be enjoyed even if you are not planning to buy anything. A short walk west and the mood shifts into Marunouchi, where office towers and wide streets create a more businesslike, big-city geometry. Tokyo Station sits nearby as both transport machine and architectural landmark, and the whole area comes into its own later in the day, when lights reflect off glass and stone and the city takes on a quietly theatrical air. This is Tokyo at its most immaculate, best experienced on foot, with time for wandering before crossing to nearby Yurakucho for *yakitori* and sake beneath the railway arches.

The

Harajuku–Omotesandō–Meiji-jingū

This area offers some of Tokyo's sharpest contrasts, but within fairly close walking distance. Meiji-jingū sits within densely wooded grounds, a memorial shrine to Emperor Meiji and Empress Shōken, approached along broad gravel paths that quickly mute the city's noise. Midweek is the sweet spot, when the shrine's calm feels genuine. Step back out to the vibrant streets of fabled Harajuku, and the mood becomes the opposite of peaceful, defined instead by fashion and people-watching. Omotesandō provides the area's elegant spine, while side streets deliver the real variety and visual spectacle, from the independent shops and cafés of Cat Street to the teen-fashion intensity of Takeshita-dōri. Nearby, Yoyogi-kōen adds breathing space, preventing the area from feeling purely commercial. Few places demonstrate Tokyo's ability to swing from reverent serenity to technicolour street style quite so convincingly.

(O) Mirrored entrance to Tokyu Plaza Omotesando Harajuku mall; (L) Crowds on Takeshita-dōri; (T) Takeshita-dōri at night

TOHO CINEMAS
楽園
SHIBUYA 109
H&M
150m
UC
Hisamitsu
サロンパス
地方競馬!
競輪!
オートレース!
ネットで馬券・車券を買うなら
オッズパーク!
Odds Park
0120-953-620
ガスト
BIC CAMERA
免税
TaxFree
LUSH
DHC Channel
DHC
YouTube Music
オフライン再生
DMM
FX
ROLA
書店

Shibuya & Daikanyama

Shibuya is built around movement, crowds and after-dark energy, and the famous scramble crossing is only the most visible expression of it. Centre Gai funnels people into a dense maze of bars and clubs, and the district's nightlife reputation is earned rather than advertised. Even the station infrastructure becomes part of the experience, with Okamoto Tarō's huge *Myth of Tomorrow* mural displayed in a connecting corridor, turning a commuter passage into an unexpected gallery. For a different rhythm, drift towards Daikanyama, where the streets feel more boutique and composed, with independent shops and a calmer café culture. Taken together, they present one of Tokyo's favourite sleights of hand: an almost-cinematic hard cut from bright noise to a softer, slower scene.

(L) The heart of Tokyo; (T) Pedestrians on iconic Shibuya crossing; (B) Signage and crowds on Shibuya Centre Gai

Shinjuku & Kabukichō

Shinjuku is Tokyo in microcosm, from high-rise ambition to tiny drinking dens. Shinjuku Station is a messy knot of terminals and subway lines, feeding in at least two million commuters a day and spitting them out through sixty exits. If you lose your bearings, head up to street level and use the Nishi-Shinjuku skyscrapers as your compass. Kabukichō, northeast of the station, is still one of the city's seedier districts, yet it's generally safe for casual wandering. The mood shifts block by block: Omoide Yokochō, squeezed against the tracks and lit by hundreds of red lanterns, is an atmospheric alley for *yakitori* spots and drinking holes. Then there's Golden Gai, just west of Hanazono-jinja – a famously cramped warren of tiny bars where postwar bohemia and late-night Tokyo still mingle, now with a younger generation keeping the scene alive. Hanazono Shrine, studded with vermilion *torii*, brings a pocket of calm to the hectic landscape and, on Sundays, a flea market. Shinjuku rewards those who stay out late and take their time heading home.

(L) A labyrinthine alley off Golden Gai; (T) Hanazono Shrine; (B) Popular izakaya bars in Omoide Yokochō

Tsukiji Outer Market & Toyosu

Tsukiji was literally built from disaster: after the Fire of the Long Sleeves in 1657, debris was used to reclaim land from the bay, giving the district its name – *tsukiji*, meaning "reclaimed land". The huge fish market is gone now, its indoor halls and famed tuna auctions shifted 2km east to Toyosu, but Tsukiji's outer market has stayed put: a dense grid of lanes heaving with grocers, pottery merchants, kitchenware sellers and the occasional stubborn fishmonger. Mornings still bring a crush of sushi-seeking visitors and the smell of the day's haul. Toyosu, by contrast, is the polar opposite: modern, efficient, popular, if slightly sterile, even as hundreds of varieties of seafood pass through daily beneath bright lights and clean lines. It is best approached as an early start and a focused mission: secure a spot for the tuna auction viewing, then linger afterwards for top-quality sushi once the market is fully awake.

(O) Beef sushi in Tsukiji market; (L) An immersive digital art installation at teamLab Planets Tokyo in Toyosu; (T) Frozen tuna going to market; (B) The new towers of Toyosu at night

Odaiba & THE Tokyo Bay waterfront

Odaiba is Tokyo's great waterfront escape: a sprawling district of reclaimed land in the bay where the city suddenly acquires sea views and open skies. The name comes from the cannon batteries built here in 1853 to deter Commodore Perry's Black Ships, but modern Odaiba is more about leisure than defence. Since development began in the late 1980s, it has become prized for something Tokyo rarely offers: seaside air and a sense of space. Start at Odaiba-hama, the man-made beach at Odaiba Seaside Park, with views of the illuminated Rainbow Bridge and an unexpected mini Statue of Liberty. From there, it's an easy hop between big, glossy distractions: Aqua City, Decks Tokyo Beach, Tokyo Joypolis and the Miraikan science museum. Come at dusk, ride the Yurikamome as it arcs towards the bridge, then end at the water's edge, watching the skyline switch on its lights.

(O) Rainbow Bridge, Odaiba; (L) A small-scale Lady Liberty; (T) The bay front at sunset

Kichijōji–Inokashira–Mitaka

Kichijōji is the sort of western Tokyo neighbourhood that makes you wonder why you ever bothered with the city centre. It's an easy place to wander around, but cut into Inokashira Park and the atmosphere turns soft-focus, with tree-shaded walks, a pleasant carp-filled lake and courting couples. In spring the whole place gets mobbed as it explodes into a cloud of pink blossoms, but outside *hanami* it remains one of the city's best pressure-release valves. Keep going and you hit Mitaka's star attraction, the utterly beguiling Ghibli Museum. Visiting feels like climbing inside the imagination of world-famous filmmaker Hayao Miyazaki, with walls of sketches, a giant clock threaded by a winding staircase and the grinning Cat-bus waiting to hijack your inner child. Book ahead, make a visit, then take the long way back through the park.

(L) Colourful Ghibli Museum

Yokohama waterfront & Chinatown

Yokohama began as a fishing village, then became one of the key treaty ports opened to foreign trade, and that international heritage still gives the city its distinctive flavour. Chinatown is the obvious draw, being Japan's largest and always busy with lively restaurants and bustling shops. It is anchored by Kantei-byō, a richly decorated shrine dedicated to the guardian deity Guan Yu, all writhing dragons and vivid colour. From there, it's a short hop to the harbourfront, where Yamashita-kōen opens onto the bay and Ōsanbashi pier hosts the city's wave-inspired international passenger terminal. Minato Mirai 21 provides the modern skyline: a mini-city built on reclaimed docklands, with the Landmark Tower's views, museums, Ferris wheel spectacle and red-brick warehouses repurposed as dining and shopping venues. Yokohama is a city best experienced on foot and by ferry, mixing history with a wash of waterfront air.

(O) The traditional ornate gate of Kantei-byō shrine;
(L) Landmark Tower; (T) Nightlife in Chinatown;
(B) The dazzling Ferris wheel on the harbourfront

Kamakura

Kamakura is a relaxed coastal town with serious historical weight, hemmed in by the sea and a ring of wooded hills. Modern Kamakura revolves around the station and the shopping streets that funnel visitors towards Tsurugaoka Hachiman-gū. The grand approach runs along Wakamiya-ōji, while nearby Komachi-dōri offers a dense run of snack stalls, souvenir shops and increasingly stylish boutiques. The shrine itself carries Minamoto clan history and a dramatic backstory, but the ponds, bridges and stages keep the precinct lively rather than solemn. Beyond the central bustle, Kamakura's real pleasure lies in walking into the hills. Hiking trails are straightforward, yet rewarding, threading through wooded scenery and connecting to temples that feel quietly secluded. Add the Daibutsu – a giant bronze Buddha – then follow one of the wooded trails between temples before hopping on the train down the coast towards Enoshima. By late afternoon, when the day-trippers peel away, Kamakura shows its best side: a quiet seaside town, far from Tokyo's intensity.

(L) Daibutsu, the famous Buddha bronze statue; (T) Sunset on the coast looking to Mount Fuji; (B) Bamboo forest

Enoshima & THE Shōnan coast

Enoshima is an easy continuation from Kamakura, reached by the rattling Enoden line and a short walk across a bridge built over what was once a sand spit. The island is compact, but it packs in enough to feel like a proper day out. Climb the busy approach lined with restaurants and souvenir stalls into the Enoshima-jinja shrine complex, spread across three linked shrines and dedicated to the guardian of sailors and fishermen. There are even escalators tunnelled through the hill-side if you'd rather save your knees. Higher up, Samuel Cocking Park, named after an English merchant who built Japan's first greenhouse here in 1880, offers gardens and views of Fuji on clear days. Paths then drop towards rocky shores and the Iwaya caves, where the walk by the waves is often more enjoyable than the caves themselves – especially late in the day, when the light softens and Mount Fuji hangs on the horizon.

(O) Mount Fuji towers over Enoshima; (L) The Enoshima lighthouse; (T) Hetsunomiya-jinja, part of the Enoshima-jinga complex

Nikkō

"Nikkō is Nippon", goes the town's slogan – only half-correct, but it's easy to see why. For many visitors, Nikkō comes close to the image of Japan they carry in their heads: a cosy mountain town where broad, tree-lined approaches lead to the UNESCO World Heritage-listed Tōshō-gū, all lacquer, detail and Tokugawa grandeur. When the senses need a rest, Futarasan-jinja's relative simplicity comes as a relief, while Taiyūin Reibyō hides among lofty pines on the hillside beyond. Step away from the shrine precincts and Nikkō gets better still: the restrained elegance of the Tamozawa Imperial Villa, then Ganman-ga-fuchi, a modest gorge with a tranquil riverside path lined by weathered Narabi-jizō statues. Push on to Chūzenji-ko for Kegon Falls, or up to Yumoto for sulphur air, lake walks and the marshes of Senjōgahara. Stay overnight – after dark, the town becomes refreshingly quiet.

(L) Shrine at Tōshō-gū; (T) The Kegon Falls; (B) An elegantly landscaped Nikko garden

Mount Takao

(T) Mount Fuji as viewed from Mount Takao

An hour west of Shinjuku, Mount Takao (600m) is Tokyo's most civilized escape route – close enough for a half-day, but green enough to clear your head. The Keiō Line drops you at Takao-san-guchi, from where you can hike up or take the cable car or chairlift to Yakuo-in, a temple founded in the eighth century and dressed up with ornate polychromatic carvings. If you're here on the second Sunday in March, the spectacular Hiwatarisai fire ritual adds a dose of theatre: priests and pilgrims march across hot coals, and visitors can follow if they trust their feet. From the temple, it's a relatively short walk to the summit, with longer trails pushing on into the Chichibu-Tama National Park. It's Tokyo's outdoors at its most accessible – a mountain excursion that still fits around a train timetable.

Kawagoe

Kawagoe is a "Little Edo" that earns the nickname once you leave the modern station area behind and reach the compact historic quarter. The town is best known for its *kurazukuri* – black, two-storey, fireproof shophouses built by merchants who grew rich trading goods along the Shingashi River and the old Kawagoe-kaidō; sixteen prime examples still line Chūō-dōri. The standout stop is Kita-in, where serene gardens surround a transplanted secondary palace from Edo Castle – the only surviving structure from Edo castle – connected by a covered wooden bridge. Nearby, the Gohyaku Rakan grove is a delightfully eccentric sight: 538 stone disciples, each with a different expression. Come in October for the grand *matsuri*, when ornate floats and costumed revellers take over the streets.

(L) Float during the Kawagoe matsuri (T) Sakura trees canopy Shingashi River; (B) Walking through the ema tunnel of wishes

Hakone

Hakone is Tokyo's classic quick-change act: in the space of a morning you can swap concrete for hot-spring steam and epic mountain views. Most visitors follow the well-established day-trip route, which is good fun and combines rides on several trains or buses, a funicular, a cable-car and a sightseeing ship across a lake. The typical itinerary runs anti-clockwise from Hakone-Yumoto, gateway to the Fuji-Hakone-Izu National Park, then over the peaks of Sōun-zan, gliding up into sulphur-seeping moonscapes where the ground looks scorched and the air carries a sharp mineral tang. You'll then drop down to the lake and hop aboard the seventeenth-century-style "galleons" for a slow cruise between the hills, with Mount Fuji sometimes appearing like a backdrop painted onto the horizon, across the length of Ashino-ko to Moto-Hakone, and back to the start. Then do Hakone properly, the way it wants to be done. Check into a *ryokan*, take a long soak, eat well and let the day blur into quietness.

(L) Taking a moment under a red torii gate at Lake Ashi, Hakone

Fuji Five Lakes

The Fuji Five Lakes region is the place to get close to Japan's defining mountain, and to see it as more than just an icon. Mount Fuji is at its most beautiful from October to May, when the summit is crowned with snow, while the climbing season runs from July to August – even if you're only coming to look rather than ascend. The lakes each have a distinct feel. Kawaguchi-ko is the busy hub and starting point for many climbers, with an easy hike up Mount Tenjō offering sweeping views. Shōji-ko is singled out as the prettiest – small and atmospheric – while Sai-ko and Motosu-ko are better suited for swimming and camping. Nearby Fuji-Yoshida is home to the striking Chureito Pagoda, whose five-storey silhouette framing Mount Fuji has become one of Japan's most celebrated views, as well as Fuji Sengen-jinja and the Yoshida Fire Festival in late August, when bonfires light up the main street. Spend a night here, and Mount Fuji stops being a backdrop and starts shaping the rhythm of the entire day.

(O) Mount Fuji framed by acer leaves; (L) Taking the cable car up the slopes in Kawaguhci-ko; (T) A prime view; (B) A solitary boat on the waters of Shōji-ko

Chūbu

Chūbu is Japan's roof and its backroads, a region where the Japan Alps dominate the skyline and onsen towns and ski resorts tuck into the valleys. Its interior holds time-honoured castle and temple towns, post-station villages on the old Nakasendō, and carpenter-built Takayama. From Kanazawa's elegant streets on the Sea of Japan to the rugged Noto coast and Sado-ga-shima's dramatic scenery, it's a region made for slow detours at any time of year.

Kanazawa

Once one of Japan's largest cities in the Edo period, Kanazawa still feels pleasantly unhurried – the sort of place that rewards wandering rather than ticking off sights. Start with Kenroku-en, a masterclass in garden-making laid out over two centuries, where sculpted pines, hillside pools and carefully engineered fountains create a landscape that never looks accidental. Slip across to the castle park, where Edo-period buildings have been rebuilt with traditional methods, then spend the rest of the day in the city's well-preserved historic districts. Nagamachi's earthen walls and narrow lanes recall the samurai era, while the Higashi Chaya District preserves the rare tradition of geisha culture outside Kyoto, with teahouses you can still step inside. Add craft culture – gold leaf, silk dyeing, Nō theatre – and a food scene built on exceptional seafood, and Kanazawa more than earns its reputation for quiet sophistication.

(L) Pink skies over the Kanazawa castle park

Noto Peninsula

Noto is the Sea of Japan coast at its most atmospheric – all rugged headlands and small fishing settlements – where it feels as though the landscape sets the tempo. In Wajima, the craft focus is lacquerware: high-quality *Wajima-nuri* sold around town, plus museums and workshops where you can watch artisans at work. Along the Okunoto coastline, the scenery turns playful and strange, with rock formations nicknamed for their silhouettes and empty stretches that make you slow down and look harder. The showstopper is Shiroyone Senmaida, where more than a thousand tiny rice terraces cling to a steep hillside as it drops towards the sea. Farming here is still done by hand, the slopes too steep for machines, and in winter the paddies glow each night with an enormous LED light display that makes the hillside glow. It's a place to experience Japan's edge-of-the-map beauty, in all its dramatic and unforgettable splendour.

(L) Ganmon Rock on the Noto Peninsula; (T) Shiroyone Senmaida's rice terraces lit up at night; (B) Hatago Iwa rock formation

Takayama

Renowned for its skilled carpenters, Takayama wears its craftsmanship lightly, but its heritage can be seen in the attractive merchant houses, shrines and temples that line its old streets. The compact core is the San-machi Suji neighbourhood: dark wooden façades, sake breweries, craft shops and cafés. Cross the Miyagawa River to Takayama Jinya, the feudal-era administrative complex built in 1615 – part residence, part working office, and unusually intimate for Japanese history. If you time it right, during the spring or autumn Takayama Matsuri, the town's festivals roll out huge *yatai* floats adorned with mechanical dolls, a striking reminder that Takayama still does tradition with real engineering. Refuel with Hida beef, a prized local wagyu, or *hōba* miso, miso grilled on a magnolia leaf with spring onions, mushrooms and other seasonal additions, then wander back into those narrow streets and let the town do the rest.

(L) Kitsune fox statue at an Inari shrine; (T) Takayama's narrow streets; (B) Nakabashi Bridge and cherry blossoms

Shirakawa-gō

(T) Shirakawa-gō showcases gasshō-zukuri houses

Even if you've seen the photographs, Shirakawa-gō still has impact: steep thatched roofs rising like clasped hands against a mountain backdrop, with a village layout that feels shaped by weather and necessity. Ogimachi is the heart of it, and while the daytime crowds can make it feel like a set, the place becomes something else entirely once the coaches leave. The best strategy is to stay overnight in one of the thatch-roofed farmhouses turned *minshuku* – a rare chance to sleep inside a building type designed to endure deep winters. Local museums and open-air collections help decode what you're seeing. The Myōzen-ji Temple Museum, once living quarters for monks, shows how the buildings worked in practice – even down to smoke from the hearth filtering through the structure to preserve wood and thatch. Across the river, the Gasshō-zukuri Minka-en open-air museum gathers relocated farmhouses into a single walkable landscape.

Kiso Valley

The Kiso Valley is where Japan's old highways still feel legible. Three of the eleven post towns (juku) that lined the Kiso-ji (Kiso road) section of the Nakasendō – Narai, Tsumago and Magome – have been preserved as virtual museums of the feudal past, and the latter two are linked by an easy two-hour hiking trail along the Nakasendō which has deservedly become one of the most popular day-hikes in Japan, as you move through a landscape of forested slopes and river valleys. The pleasure is in the transitions, where you leave a station or road behind and suddenly find yourself on a path edged by trees, stone and low wooden buildings. In towns like Magome and Tsumago, traditional facades and compact streets make it easy to imagine the rhythm of travellers arriving on foot. Narai adds a different flavour – longer, more linear, with an extended main street that feels built for traffic that came by sandals, not engines. None of these places are very big, which is part of the appeal.

(O) Magome's picturesque townscape;
(L) A kimono-wearing woman in the old town of Tsumago;
(T) Traditional houses in Narai; (B) The Kiso Valley

Matsumoto

Matsumoto is a gateway city that doesn't behave like one. Yes, it's the jumping-off point for the Japanese Alps, but it's also the sort of place you'll want to linger for longer. The centrepiece is Matsumoto-jō – Crow Castle – brooding black against its moat, one of the country's few intact medieval wooden castles and deservedly a National Treasure. Inside, steep staircases climb to the top floor, passing displays of weaponry and artefacts, with views over town and the mountain skyline waiting at the top. Beyond the castle, Matsumoto's appeal lies in its riverside neighbourhoods. Nakamachi-dōri is lined with striking black-and-white-walled buildings that now hold craft shops and cafés, including the beautifully restored Kurassic-kan, a former sake brewery with a dramatic interior. On the other bank, Nawate-dōri is livelier and more playful, a pedestrian lane of stalls and snack stops. Add strong museums – from ukiyo-e to Yayoi Kusama – and Matsumoto becomes a place in its own right, much more than just a stopover.

(L) Majestic Crow Castle

Nagano & Zenkō-ji

Nagano is a modern, compact city with an old soul still accessible at the top of its main street. Walk up Chūō-dōri and you'll arrive at Zenkō-ji, a temple complex that has drawn pilgrims since the seventh century. It was founded to house a statue believed to be among the first Buddhist images to reach Japan, and its appeal has always been unusually broad – welcoming followers of all sects and never excluding women, with leadership alternating between Tendai and Jōdo schools. Join the pilgrims feeling their way in the darkness beneath the main hall, searching for the so-called "key to paradise", and the place becomes physical and intimate. The approach is intriguing in itself, with snack stalls, the Daihongan nunnery, imposing gates and the movement from ordinary city life into something older and stranger. The pre-dawn morning service brings the complex to life with chanting, drums and blessings.

(O) Zenkō-ji temple; (L) Nagano city at dusk;
(T) The O-Asaji morning ceremony at Zenkō-ji

Obuse

Obuse is an idyllic pocket of rural Nagano that combines a strong artistic heritage with a love of good food and drink. It's closely tied to Katsushika Hokusai, whose late-life work gives the town an artistic backbone. Start in the centre and you'll quickly find the Hokusai Museum, where waves, dragons and phoenixes hint at the restless energy of his imagination, then step into the quieter atmosphere of the Takai Kōzan Memorial Museum, the former home of his patron, rich with eccentric drawings and calligraphy. The town's most memorable art sits slightly beyond the centre at Gansho-in, where Hokusai painted a dramatic phoenix across the temple ceiling in a lush foothill setting. Between sights, Obuse leans into the pleasures of tasting. Local breweries pour sake, including traditional cedar-barrel styles, while local sweetmakers turn chestnuts into the town's signature treat.

(L) Cherry blossom in full bloom, Obuse; (T) Sake bottles at the Masuichi Ichimura Sake Brewery; (B) Grasses in Obuse park

Kamikōchi

Kamikōchi is famous, and in peak season it can feel like it, but it still has a geunine impact – a mountain valley whose beauty is immediate. Its best moments, however, are found by heading just a little beyond the obvious places. The trail along the Azusa River strings together classic scenes: Taishō-ike, a glassy pond formed when a 1915 eruption dammed the river, with dead tree trunks still rising from the water; marshy boardwalk trails; and the photogenic Kappa-bashi suspension bridge at the village centre. But hike further north and the crowds drop away on the route to Myōjin-ike, a quiet pool with a small shrine whose atmosphere is deepened by its role in an annual October festival. Kamikōchi's history as a mountaineering base is tied to Walter Weston, who helped popularize the Japan Alps but worried about growing visitor numbers. The solution is simple: arrive early, walk beyond the bottlenecks, and, if you can, stay overnight so the valley has time to reset.

(L, T) Kamikōchi national park in autumn; (B) Myōjin-ike and its shrine

Hakuba Valley

(T) Snow drifts in Hakuba's valley

Hakuba is best known for winter, but it's really a mountain valley for all seasons – a resort where you can ski hard, hike and cycle in the summer, and indulge in long, restorative evenings. The area has an international feel, reflected in the easy-going mix of cafés and bars around the station and beyond. In the evenings, the social centre can be as simple as a log-cabin café-bar near the station, serving pizza and pulling in a friendly crowd, or a brewpub up by the Iwatake ski area pouring beer made with spring water that began as snow on the surrounding slopes. Beyond its scenery and social life, the valley is also a convenient base for exploring neighbouring mountain regions, allowing you to range widely during the day and return somewhere relaxed and low-key each evening. At its best, Hakuba offers a combination Japan doesn't always deliver in one place: big mountain scenery, good infrastructure and enough character that you never feel trapped inside a resort bubble.

大湯
24h SECURITY SYSTEM IN OPERATION
防犯カメラ作動中
監視「録画」しています
頭上注意
watch your head
女湯
Lady's
賽銭

Nozawa Onsen

Nozawa Onsen doesn't feel like a resort that happens to have a village attached. It's a village of four thousand people that has been sitting at the base of Kenashi-yama for over a thousand years, and the onsen come with the territory. The place is built for a simple hot spring routine: pad along narrow, twisting streets, duck into one of the thirteen free bathhouses, then step back out into sharp mountain air. Start with Ō-yu, a temple-like wooden bathhouse in the centre, complete with statues of the Buddha of Healing and two attendant bodhisattvas, and water so hot it makes you pay attention to your body and the rituals. In January, the Dōso-jin fire festival turns the village into a full-noise blaze of tradition. In winter the slopes do the rest, backed up by tasty onsen *manjū* – steamed buns filled with sweet red bean paste – from street vendors, and a refreshing beer at the Libushi microbrewery.

(L) Ō-yu bathhouse is the largest and grandest in the resort

Jigokudani–Shiga Kōgen

Many Japanese ski areas are compact by international standards; Shiga Kōgen is a notable exception. Mammoth and winter-only, it's a linked chain of eighteen resorts strung out along the Shiga plateau in the Jōshin'etsu Kōgen National Park, with enough terrain variety to keep you busy for days. A single lift pass covers the entire network, which makes it excellent value if you've got the legs for it. Anyone short of time should head straight for the northern end – Okushiga-kōgen and Yakebitai-yama – both strong on long, fast cruising and with the bragging rights of having hosted the slalom events at the 1998 Winter Olympics. Even the approach feels like part of the experience: buses climb up from Yudanaka via a dramatic mountain pass, skirting Jigokudani Monkey Park on the way. Pick your base carefully and you can ski big without spending half the day on logistics.

(O) Transport to the slopes; (L) "March of Rime", or rime frost, also known as "snow monsters"; (T) Tatami room in the ski resort; (B) Macaque at Jigokudani Monkey Park

CHŪBU

Niigata

Niigata is often treated as transit – a port city people pass through on the way to Sado Island – but it has enough personality to justify a pause. Set on the banks of the Shinano River, it's a likeable place with a quieter energy than Japan's headline cities, rewarding travellers who enjoy small discoveries, whether that's museums that don't shout for attention, older neighbourhoods with traces of the city's past, or a food-and-drink culture that's a genuine reason to linger. Niigata is particularly associated with excellent *nihonshū* (sake), and this is the place to explore that reputation properly, as part of how the city eats and relaxes. For travellers moving quickly through the country, Niigata presents a welcome change of rhythm from many other areas, in a walkable port city where sea views, serious sake, market food and easy-going neighbourhoods reveal a quieter side of urban Japanese life.

(L) One of Niigata's peaceful gardens; (T) Rice terraces in winter; (B) Bottles of sake for sale

Sado-ga-shima

Sado feels like an island with several histories layered on top of each other – working-port roughness, rice-field calm, remote headlands, and the long shadow of exile and mining wealth. The north is where the drama sits. Aikawa was once a booming mining town, its gold and silver feeding shogunal coffers, and while the mines are no longer active, their story feels tangible at Sado Kinzan. Walk the Edo-era Sōdayū Tunnel and you get a sense of the brutal working conditions, recreated with animatronic miners, while the Meiji-era Dōyū Tunnel reveals a different scale and ends with striking views of a mountain literally split by extraction. Beyond Aikawa, the coastline turns wilder, best explored by car, especially when winter snow closes the mountain passes. Elsewhere on the island, Ryōtsu still carries the feel of a working ferry town – slightly weathered, uncommercialized and set between the sea and an oyster-farming lake.

(O) The vivid red bridge connecting the islets of Yajima and Kyoujima; (L) Sado's Five Story Pagoda; (T) A model depicting the making of gold coins

Nagoya

Nagoya doesn't try to charm, which is part of its appeal. Rebuilt after wartime air raids, it's a modern metropolis of broad roads and high-rises where business comes first – as the home of Toyota and the culture of *monozukuri*, Japan's philosophy of craftsmanship and manufacturing excellence. That said, it's far from dull if you know where to look. The city's partially restored castle, originally ordered by Tokugawa Ieyasu, anchors its history, and the reconstructed Honmaru Palace beside it is the real draw, painstakingly rebuilt with traditional techniques and filled with sumptuous painted screens. Elsewhere, Nagoya leans confidently into modern attractions, from a science museum with the world's largest planetarium to museums devoted to industry and rail technology, including the futuristic SCMaglev and Railway Park. It also makes a strong base for regional day trips, with excellent transport links and an international airport. Nagoya is not pretending to be "traditional Japan". Instead, it shows the country's contemporary, industrious side.

(L) Nagoya castle; (T) The dazzling entrance to the city's Osu shopping arcade; (B) Modern features of Nagoya

稲荷大神
奉
納

Kansai

Kansai is where Japan first took root. From the rice-growing plains around Osaka and Kyoto to the old Yamato heartland, it is imbued with the region's deep pride in having shaped the nation's story. Here, Kyoto and Nara still carry the weight of imperial history and traditional arts, while Osaka answers with neon, street food and nightlife. Add castles, pilgrimage mountains and forested sacred routes, and few places bring Japan's past and present together so vividly.

Kyoto: Higashiyama *& THE* temple-walk cityscape

Higashiyama is Kyoto at street level: a cityscape stitched together by slopes, lanes and temple gates, where the best sights reveal themselves through a walk rather than a single stop. Start around the broad *torii* by Heian-jingū and drift east along the Biwa Canal to Murin-an, a delightful retreat created by Meiji power-broker Yamagata Aritomo – all meandering streams, ponds and lawns. From here it's a short climb to Nanzen-ji, one of Kyoto's most important Zen complexes. Don't skip Konchi-in's dry garden, credited to Kobori Enshū, where crane and tortoise rocks play out a stone allegory of longevity. Then take in the looming San-mon gate, and the Hōjō's Kanō Tanyū screens depicting tigers among bamboo. Finish the day on the Philosopher's Path, a 2km canal-side stroll from just north of Nanzen-ji to Ginkaku-ji, especially beautiful during cherry blossom season.

(O) Traditonal kimono attire at Yasaka Pagoda; (L) A rickshaw tour of the temples; (T) A stone bridge reflected in still pond waters

Fushimi Inari & THE Fushimi sake district

Fushimi reveals a different side of Kyoto – a district of canals and low-rise streets lined with wooden houses and generations-old sake breweries, seemingly made for an unhurried wander or leisurely bike ride. The headline sight, though, is Fushimi Inari Taisha – the head shrine of the Inari cult, dedicated to the god of rice and sake. The mistake is lingering around the main sanctuary. The real experience starts in the forest, on the 4km maze of paths that climbs Inari-san beneath more than 10,000 vermilion *torii*, sometimes packed so tightly they can cut out most light even on bright days. Each gate is an offering, the donor's name inscribed in black; foxes stand guard as Inari's messengers, their association with rice and harvests making them one of the shrine's defining symbols. Climb for the views, descend for a cup of tea and *inari-zushi* (fried tofu pouches filled with rice), then finish back among the breweries, where the local logic – rice becomes sake – feels neatly complete.

(O) Approaching Fushimi Inari Taisha; (L) A guardian fox; (T) In the shrine; (B) Sake casks

Arashiyama & Sagano

Arashiyama works best as a half-day that turns into a full day once you stop trying to rush it. The river scenery is the anchor, with walks that follow the water and draw you into quieter corners beyond the first busy streets. The bamboo grove is the famous image, and it is genuinely striking, but it rewards good timing and an early start if you want atmosphere rather than crowds. Beyond the grove, the district opens out into hillside gardens and small temple precincts where the mood shifts quickly from bustle to calm. The best way to experience Arashiyama is to simply keep moving. Cross the bridge, follow the river and climb gently into Sagano's lanes, then finish with a slow return as the light fades over the water.

(L) Arashiyama's famous bamboo grove

Downtown Kyoto

If much of Kyoto is about temples and gardens, downtown Kyoto is about how the city lives and eats. Nishiki-kōji has served as "Kyoto's kitchen" for centuries, and the covered lane is still a tight, lively corridor of specialist stalls, from *yuba* (tofu skin, often served simply with soy sauce and wasabi) and freshly grilled seafood to assorted pickles and vegetables that reflect the city's obsession with seasonality. The market is also home to specialist *mochi* vendors and some of the best matcha and black sesame ice cream in the city. There is great pleasure in browsing, tasting and letting the market set your pace, then stepping out into the surrounding streets where *machiya* townhouses and small temples keep the area from feeling purely commercial. As evening falls, the mood intensifies along Pontochō – a narrow, lantern-lit alley running beside the Kamo-gawa, long associated with Kyoto's geisha culture, and improbably atmospheric for somewhere so central.

(L) Woman in traditonal geisha dress; (T) Nishiki-kōji traders; (B) Relaxing on the riverside

Nara

(T) Lighting incense at Tōdai-ji

Nara's great charm is that its most important sites sit within real parkland, with deer roaming through lawns and ancient woods, as if the city never fully replaced the forest. Tōdai-ji is the centrepiece, both for its scale and for the presence of the Great Buddha within, a sight that still feels monumental even if you arrive expecting it. The wider Nara-kōen area makes the visit enjoyable as a day of walking rather than a single stop, with shrine paths, lantern-lined approaches and quiet corners where the crowds fall away. The old town beyond the park has a gentler pace than Kyoto or Osaka, and it's easy to spend an extra hour simply drifting between small artisan shops and backstreets. Nara feels like a foundational place, where early Japan remains visible in both landscape and layout.

Hōryū-ji & Ikaruga

Hōryū-ji sits in the quieter Ikaruga area southwest of Nara, a calm setting that forms part of its impact. The complex is celebrated for holding the world's oldest surviving wooden building, yet the experience of being here isn't about a single headline fact. It's about standing among structures that carry the atmosphere of early Japanese Buddhism, with timber, tiled roofs and courtyards that feel designed for devotion rather than spectacle. The surrounding neighbourhood keeps the visit grounded, with fields and low-rise streets that make the temple's age feel even more striking. Combining a visit here with one to Nara makes sense, but Hōryū-ji offers a different register: less crowded, more contemplative, and better suited to a slow exploration. This encounter with history doesn't require specialist knowledge, only patience and attention.

(L) Hōryū-ji is home to the oldest surviving wooden building in the world;
(T) Hōryū-ji i pagoda and shrine; (B) The Great Lecture Hall

Uji

Uji is Kyoto's quieter companion, a riverside town where culture and landscape are inextricably tied to tea. The area has supplied Kyoto with tea for centuries, and the town still feels shaped by that tradition, from teashops to the green hush of nearby fields. Byōdō-in is the classic visit, originally an aristocratic villa before becoming a temple in the eleventh century. The Phoenix Hall, set beside the pond, is the moment that makes you stop, its reflection restoring something of the Pure Land vision the builders intended. Make time for a riverside walk and a traditional tea ceremony, or stop into one of the many teahouses for a bowl of matcha paired with traditional sweets and you'll get a sense of Kyoto elegance without the pressure of adjacent crowds.

(L) Byōdō-in

Osaka Minami

Minami is Osaka turned up to full volume, and the best way to experience it is to arrive hungry and stay out late. Dōtombori runs along the canal in a blaze of neon and noise, with restaurants treating spectacle as part of the meal and street snacks keeping you moving. The area is dense enough that a short wander can turn into hours, especially once you slip off the main drag into backstreets where tiny bars and standing eateries feel more local than performative. Osaka's pride in its food culture is palpable here, and it rarely feels precious. It's quick, funny and unapologetically sociable. Minami's appeal is not about a single sight, but an atmosphere: a place where the city's identity plays out nightly, over skewers, beer and good conversation.

(L, T, B) Neon lights, kitsch and colour in Minami's lively dining and entertainment streets

Osaka Castle Park & THE city's historic core

Osaka-jō is less a relic than a symbol, and the park around it consciously gives the site room to breathe. The castle's story is tangled with power struggles, rebuilding and survival, and even though the main tower is a reconstruction (with its own lift inside, as well as one outside – head up to the eighth floor for a panoramic view of the city and castle grounds), the setting still conveys ambition through moats, stonework and wide approaches. Enter through the main gates and you begin to understand the scale of the original fortress, built to dominate. The surrounding parkland makes it easy to turn the visit into a longer walk, and the nearby museums add depth, particularly if you want context beyond the main tower. The best moments come when you step back and look at the castle framed by water and trees, letting the city's skyline sit behind it.

(O) Osaka's castle; (L) Ornate golden motifs adorn the castle; (T) A boat ride on the castle's inner moat

Kōya-san

(T) Shrines in Kōya-san's sacred mountains

Kōya-san is a mountain town that feels like a deliberate withdrawal from ordinary life. The journey up helps, and once you arrive the best decision is to stay overnight in a temple lodging, where early prayers and vegetarian *shōjin-ryōri* meals are the order of the day. These temple meals are carefully prepared without meat, fish or strong seasonings, built around seasonal vegetables, tofu, mountain herbs and subtle broths, often presented as a sequence of small, balanced dishes. The main sights in the area are spread between the Garan precinct and Okunoin Cemetery, whose forest paths are lined with thousands of memorials and tombs, leading to Kōbō Daishi's mausoleum glowing with lantern light. Even in daylight, the atmosphere is unusually hushed, shaped by cedar shade and the steady flow of pilgrims. Here, there is no need to rush – Kōya-san rewards slow movement.

Kumano Kodō

The Kumano Kodō is less a single trail than a web of ancient routes threading through the Kii Peninsula's isolated mountains, where forest, waterfalls and village life set the pace as much as spiritual tradition does. It grew out of a gradual blending of Shintō and Buddhism and was strengthened by imperial pilgrimages from the tenth century, with the Kumano Sanzan shrines acting as the spiritual anchors. Kumano Hongū Taisha is the sacred centre, rebuilt on higher ground after the devastating flood of 1889, with a gigantic *torii* now marking the former site at Oyunohara. Look out for the *yatagarasu*, the three-legged crow associated with divine guidance, and keep walking. Stone paths, roadside *oji* shrines and the sound of water in ravines make the journey feel alive, with onsen towns such as Yunomine offering the perfect end to a day on foot.

(L) Pagoda on a Kumano Kodō trail; (T) Kumano Hongū Taisha; (B) Trekking in dense forest on the pilgrimage route

Himeji

Himeji-jō is the castle that makes you reconsider what a fortress can be. The present complex of moats, thick defensive walls, keeps and connecting corridors dates from the early seventeenth century, although there has been a fortress in the town since around 1346. Its white gables and layered roofs have earned it the "White Heron" nickname, but the beauty of the building is never separate from its defensive intelligence. As you move through gates and zigzagging approaches, the design feels purposeful, guiding attackers into exposed positions while the keep rises in controlled stages above. Inside, timber staircases guide you upwards, and the views from the top underline why the site mattered strategically. Himeji's impact lies in this combination of grandeur and survival. It endured when many other castles didn't, and it still feels complete, not reduced to fragments. Combine it with a trip to the nearby Kōko-en gardens to shift focus from martial power to cultivated calm, a satisfying contrast within a short walk.

(L) Himeji-jō at night

Kōbe harbour & Kitano

The distinctive character found in Kōbe comes from the city's location, squeezed between mountains and sea, and from the history that arrived here by ship. Kitano, on the hillside above Sannomiya, holds the city's foreign residences from the port-opening era, a pocket of streets where the architecture hints at Kōbe's outward-looking past. Down by the water, the harbourfront tells a different story, one of trade, reinvention and resilience after the 1995 earthquake, with memorial elements that keep that history present. A short ride or walk can take you from bay air to steep streets, and that shift is part of the appeal. Kōbe is also a city of views. Take in the skyline from higher ground, then come back down to explore Chinatown's lanes and enjoy the waterfront evening light. Modern and international, Kōbe is distinctly itself, and best explored on foot.

(O) Sunset over Kōbe Port Tower; (L) Waterfront evening stroll; (T) The harbour's Ferris wheel; (B) Boats in harbour

Kinosaki Onsen

Kinosaki Onsen is built around a simple, deeply satisfying ritual: change into a *yukata*, slip on wooden *geta*, and wander from bath to bath through a compact town that seems designed for evening strolling. The canal lined with willows and *ryokan* façades provides the scenery, but the real pleasure is how the whole place participates. Lean into the *soto-yu* circuit – seven public bathhouses, each with its own supposed luck – and the experience stops feeling like sightseeing and starts feeling like a nightly habit. Begin with Kō no Yu, the oldest, tied to a stork legend and a little quieter for it, then switch to Gosho no Yu, with an entrance styled after Kyoto's Imperial Palace and a two-level *rotemburo*. Finish at Sato no Yu, practically in the station, for a modern soak with jet and steam baths – and views over town from the third-floor outdoor bath.

(O) Wearing at tradtional kimono at Kinosaki Onsen;
(L) Geta, traditional wooden sandals, lined up;
(T) Kinosaki Onsen blanketed by snow

Ise-jingū & Ise–Shima

Ise-jingū unfolds through long cedar-lined approaches and gravel paths where sound drops away, each *torii* marking a clear shift deeper into the shrine's inner world. The shrine complex is split into two main sanctuaries, and the experience is as much about approach as arrival, watching the rhythm of visitors at prayer and letting the quiet settle in. Ise also understands pilgrimage in a practical, enjoyable way. Oharai-machi and Okage-yokochō provide the lively counterpoint, with local food, craft shops and a sense of tradition kept in use rather than preserved at a distance. Beyond Ise, the Shima Peninsula shifts the mood to coast and coves, an easy extension into bays and inlets that feel a world away from Kyoto's bustling lanes. For a final flourish, take a boat out on Ago-wan, where the cultured-pearl industry and the tradition of *ama* women divers give Shima a quietly industrious, salt-air atmosphere.

(O) Ise-jingū is Japan's most sacred Shinto shrine; (T) Shinto priests; (B) Uji-bashi Bridge

大発

Chūgoku

Chūgoku sits in western Honshū, between Kyūshū and the Kansai heartland, with two coasts that feel almost like different countries. The industrial San'yō belt runs along the Shinkansen but opens onto the Inland Sea, scattered with islands. To the north, San-in is quieter, with castle towns, shrines and remote landscapes. Between them lie Hiroshima's memorials, Miyajima's *torii* gate and Onomichi's hillside temple paths, each offering insight on the region's rich history.

Hiroshima Peace Memorial Park & museum district

Hiroshima carries a weight that is impossible to ignore, yet its centre is a calm, modern city that naturally slows your pace. Peace Memorial Park sits on the delta island where the Ōta-gawa splits, laid out as an open green spine of monuments and water leading towards the museum. The A-bomb Dome, the skeletal remains of the former Industrial Promotion Hall, stands close to the hypocentre of the 1945 atomic bombing and still feels startling against the surrounding city streets. The Peace Memorial Museum deepens the visit with a clear, direct narrative of the bomb's impact and its human cost, and most people find they spend longer there than expected. Walk back through the park afterwards, reflecting at the deeply moving Children's Peace Monument, which depicts a young girl standing atop an elongated dome, holding aloft a giant origami crane. Its base is always festooned in multicoloured garlands of origami cranes.

(O) Peace Memorial Park; (L) Folded origami art at the Children's Peace Monument; (T) Exhibits at the Hiroshima National Peace Memorial Hall for the Atomic Bomb Victims

Miyajima

(T) Miyajima's famous torii

Miyajima's first impression is unmistakable: Itsukushima-jinja's vermilion *torii* rising from the water, with the shrine's buildings appearing to float at high tide. The shrine's setting is central to its power: rather than standing apart from the landscape, its halls, corridors and ceremonial spaces seem to merge with the sea, mountains and sky. It's an iconic spectacle that lives long in the mind, but the rest of the island rewards anyone who keeps walking. The village streets near the ferry are busy with shops and snacks, yet the atmosphere shifts quickly once you head towards the trails and temple precincts beyond. The climb to Mount Misen, on foot or by ropeway, brings a wilder feel and wide Inland Sea views, with forest paths that make the island's scale feel larger than it looks on a map. Time it well and you can catch a glimpse of Miyajima in a quieter light.

Okayama & Kōrakuen

Okayama is the city; Kōrakuen is its star attraction. The capital of Okayama-ken is an easy, manageable stop on western Honshū's San-yō coast, useful as a base for Kurashiki, Inujima and Inland Sea excursions, but it has pleasures of its own, ranging from the broad Momotarō-dōri and the covered Omotechō-shōtengai arcade to the tree-lined Nishigawa Greenway canal and the black-walled Okayama-jō, or "Crow Castle", around which the city developed in the Edo period. Kōrakuen, twenty minutes' walk east of the station, occupies a comma-shaped island in a curve of the Asahi-gawa. Laid out in 1686 by Lord Ikeda Tsunamasa, it is acclaimed as one of Japan's great gardens, notable for its unusually broad lawns, artificial lakes, islands and hills, with Okayama-jō folded neatly into the view. Together, they make Okayama more than a transit stop – the city provides the framework for exploration, while Kōrakuen provides the reason to linger.

(L, T, B) In the beautifully landscaped Kōrakuen garden, home to the black Okayama-jō

Kurashiki

Kurashiki, 18km southwest of Okayama, is one of western Honshū's most rewarding small-town stops, popular as a day trip but better appreciated overnight. Its modern approach gives little away, but ten minutes south of the station the streets settle into the beautifully preserved Bikan district, where black-and-white merchant houses and old storehouses line a willow-fringed canal. The town prospered in the Edo period through trade in rice and rush reeds, and that mercantile past still gives the old quarter its substance. Today the warehouses hold inns, cafés, craft shops and galleries, with the Ōhara Museum of Art the standout cultural draw, not least for the surprise of its Neoclassical façade amid the canal-side townscape. During the day, especially in summer, Bikan can all feel a bit too busy with tourists. Stay the night, however, and an early-morning or evening stroll along its its quieter lanes, old houses and waterside paths can be quite magical.

(L) Travelling by canal in Kurashiki

Tomonoura

Tomonoura sits at the tip of the Numakuma Peninsula, looking out across one of the loveliest stretches of the Inland Sea. Narrow lanes twist through old warehouses, shrines and temple slopes, while fishing boats still gather around the horseshoe-shaped harbour, much as they did when Edo-period trading vessels paused here to wait for a favourable tide. The town's sense of continuity with its past is its great charm. Locals sell prawns, crabs and sea bream near the water, anglers linger along the seawalls, and the tiled roofs rise gently up towards hilltop viewpoints. Its atmosphere has not gone unnoticed: Hayao Miyazaki spent time here while working on *Ponyo*, and the town later appeared in *The Wolverine*. For the best bearings, climb to the ruins of Taigashima-jō or visit Fukuzen-ji, where the Taichōrō reception hall opens onto a celebrated view over the islands. A five-minute ferry ride brings you to forested Sensui-jima, adding an easy escape into wilder scenery.

(L) Seacraft tied up in Tomonoura port; (T) Sensui-jima at night; (B) View over Tomonoura

Onomichi

(T) Looking out over Onomichi from Tennei-ji temple

Onomichi is one of the San'yō coast's most characterful ports, rough-edged in places but all the better for it. Its waterfront faces Mukai-shima across a narrow channel, while immediately behind the town the land rises steeply into wooded slopes scattered with temples, stairways and old houses. The best thing to do here is wander through the covered arcade, along back lanes, and up the signposted temple walk that links many of Onomichi's 25 temples. Senkō-ji, reached either on foot or by ropeway, gives the classic view back over the town, harbour and Inland Sea. The town also has a strong film connection, from Ozu's *Tokyo Story* to the work of local director Ōbayashi Nobuhiko, whose camera loved its vertiginous streets. Onomichi is not only atmospheric in itself, but also the northern gateway to the Shimanami Kaidō, the island-hopping cycling route to Imabari on Shikoku, making it a natural base for exploring the Inland Sea.

Shimanami Kaidō

The Shimanami Kaidō is one of the great journeys across the Inland Sea, linking Onomichi on Honshū with Imabari on Shikoku by way of six major islands and a chain of spectacular bridges. The full route runs for around 60km along the Nishi-Seto Expressway, though cyclists follow their own carefully designed lanes and ramps, with wide views opening over fishing ports, citrus groves and glittering channels of water. It can be ridden in a single long day, but there is no real need to hurry. The pleasure lies in breaking the journey, dropping down into island villages, stopping for seafood or ice cream, and lingering on Ikuchi-jima or Ōmi-shima. The bridges are part of the drama, from the Tatara Ōhashi to the 4km Kurushima-Kaikyō, yet the route is a pleasure because it feels like more than an engineering feat. It is a slow, salt-air crossing through the softer side of western Japan.

(L, T) Kurushima Kaikyo First Bridge at dusk and in daylight; (B) A cycle route with a view

Izumo Taisha & THE Shimane coast hinterland

The Shimane coast hinterland feels close to the old mythic heart of Japan, with Izumo Taisha its most powerful focus. Set in coastal foothills, this grand Shintō shrine is second in importance only to Ise and is said to host Japan's eight million deities each November, when the rest of the country marks the "month without gods" and Izumo celebrates the "month with gods". The approach is part of the spell, leading from Izumo Taisha-mae Station through *torii* gates and along the pine-lined Seki-no-Baba to the shrine at the foot of Mount Yakumo. Within the grounds, giant *shimenawa* ropes, daily ceremonies and glimpses of priests among small forest shrines give the place a lived-in sacredness. Nearby, the Shimane Museum of Ancient Izumo adds useful context, while Hinomisaki, 9km northwest, opens the landscape out to cliffs, beaches, a bright shrine and a white stone lighthouse above the sea.

(O) A shrine on sacred coastline; (L) Partaking in Kamiari festival, a traditional Japanese shinto event, at Izumo Taisha; (T) A shrine detail

Adachi Museum of Art

The Adachi Museum of Art sits in a rural pocket near Yasugi, out of the way enough to make the journey feel deliberate. The art collection is respectable rather than unforgettable, though it includes important modern Japanese works by Yokoyama Taikan and ceramics by Kawai Kanjirō and Kitaōji Rosanjin. The real reason to come, however, is the garden. Created by the museum's founder, Adachi Zenkō, its six separate landscapes are kept in almost unnerving order, every stone, leaf and stretch of raked gravel held in place. You cannot walk through them, which is part of the point; instead, the route through the museum frames each view from corridors, glass walls and tatami rooms. At times the gardens appear less like scenery than painted scrolls brought into three dimensions, especially in autumn. Remote, controlled and quietly theatrical, this is one of western Honshū's most memorable detours.

(O, L, T, B) Exemplary landscaping at the Adachi Museum of Art's celebrated garden

御神燈

御神燈

Shikoku

Shikoku is Japan at its most unhurried, a beautiful island of mountain roads, temple paths, rural valleys and small, friendly cities. Though linked to Honshū by bridges, it still feels pleasingly separate, shaped by the 88-temple pilgrimage, historic castles, hot springs, traditional crafts and the wild Pacific coast. Its rewards are often quiet ones, found in slow travel, local food, island views and a lingering sense of old Japan.

Naoshima

(T) In Lee Ufan Museum's grounds

Naoshima is the liveliest focus of the Inland Sea's art-island circuit, where fishing villages, sheltered beaches and bold contemporary architecture sit within easy reach of one another. Benesse's long-running art project has transformed the island without quite overwhelming it, bringing Tadao Ando-designed galleries, outdoor sculptures and large-scale installations to a place that still feels small and sea-bound. Around Gotanji Beach, the Benesse House Museum, Chichū Art Museum and Lee Ufan Museum make the strongest draw, with works by Monet, James Turrell, Walter de Maria and major postwar artists set against concrete, light and views of the water. Over in Honmura, the Art House Project turns old wooden homes, a temple and a shrine into intimate artworks, while Miyanoura adds Shinrō Ōtake's exuberant public bath, I♥湯 (or Naoshima Bathhouse "I Love Yu").

Teshima

The island of Teshima is lush, industrious, and quietly odd in the best way. Fishing boats and dairy farms keep it grounded, while a scatter of art sites sit in the green folds between Ieura and Karato. The centrepiece is the Teshima Art Museum, a concrete shell open to the elements on the edge of a rice terrace. From outside it looks like a UFO; inside, take your shoes off and watch small springs of water erupt from the floor and creep into mobile puddles as wind whistles through the roof openings. If that feels too serene, reset at Teshima Yokoo House, an abrupt shock of pop-culture collage. A carp pond runs under Perspex floors, a 14m-high tower is plastered with 900 postcards of waterfalls, and even the outhouse installations demand attention. Rent a bike at the port and put it all together at your own pace, with the shuttle bus as backup.

(L) The unusual shape of Teshima Art Museum; (T) Surreal art exhibit; (B) The museum's embedded structure

Shōdoshima

Shōdoshima is a mini-Shikoku with sea views, steep green hills and a slightly self-aware streak of Mediterranean cosplay. Terraced olive groves come with a whitewashed windmill and mock-Grecian ruins at Olive-kōen, and a connection to Studio Ghibli's *Kiki's Delivery Service* (directed by Hayao Miyazaki), which drew inspiration from the island's landscapes. Tonoshō's old quarter takes the mood back to Edo Japan, its Meiro no Machi lanes laid out as a defensive maze against pirates and still atmospheric enough to get pleasantly lost in. The island's cultural heart is *Nijūshi no Hitomi*, a tear-jerking story of a teacher and her pupils set here between the 1920s and 1950s, with Eigamura's fake village and Tanoura's original schoolhouse adding a film-set tang. For something earthier, head southeast to Yamaroku, where soy sauce ferments for two years in century-old wooden barrels under the eye of a fifth-generation soy master.

(L) Windmill on Shōdoshima

Takamatsu & Ritsurin-kōen

Takamatsu is Shikoku's most approachable gateway, the sort of place that wins you over between trains and ferries. Its must-do is Ritsurin-kōen, a garden built for lingering rather than ticking off. Start at the East Gate and meander through the South Garden's lakes and islands, then pause at Kikugetsu-tei, the Scooping the Moon teahouse, where matcha comes with a perfectly framed view over Nanko. Cross into the North Garden for a more natural feel, duck ponds and pines trained into improbable shapes, including the crane-and-turtle black pine, Tsurukame-matsu. Back in town, Tamamo-kōen holds the ruins of Takamatsu-jō, once one of Japan's great sea-protected fortresses, its moats still doing the atmospheric work. When hunger hits, follow the locals into the central arcades for *sanuki* udon and fresh seafood.

(O) Visiting Takamatsu's temples; (L) Boating in Ritsurin-kōen; (T) Takamatsu-jō; (B) Takamatsu's skyline

Kotohira

Kotohira is the kind of place that makes you earn the view. The whole town tilts towards Kotohira-gū, better known as Kompira-san, one of Japan's major Shintō pilgrimage sites, pulling in millions of visitors a year. The climb is the point: 1,368 steps through a mainly wooden hillside complex, past stone lanterns and the five red-painted Gonin Byakushō stalls, then on towards the Hon-gū, where priests rustle along raised corridors. If you've still got the lungs for it, push up to the Oku-sha and look out for the cartoonish Tengu carved into the rocks. Between stages, there are sly diversions: the serene Omote Shoin reception hall with Maruyama Ōkyo screens, and an open-air gallery of ship offerings that nods to Kompira's seafarers' past. Back at street level, reward yourself with *sanuki* udon or a stop at the Kinryō Sake Museum, where brewing has been happening on the same spot since 1616.

(L, T) Kotohira-gū; (B) Traditional wooden prayer tablets in the shrine

Iya Valley

Deep in Shikoku's mountainous heart, the Iya Valley still trades on remoteness. Highway and rail plunge into the spectacular Ōboke Gorge, carved by the sparkling Yoshino-gawa, with vertiginous mountains that can even be coated in snow. In 1185, defeated Taira warriors used this landscape as a bolt hole, swapping swords for farm tools and building thatch-roofed cottages on steep slopes. The modern valley has its share of concrete and depopulation, yet the special atmosphere hangs on – locals like to call it the Tibet of Japan. Come for the vine bridges, especially Iya no Kazura-bashi, a survivor of Taira times, now reinforced with discreet steel cables, or the quieter Oku-Iya Nijū Kazura-bashi deeper in. Then get under the surface. Visit Chiiori, a beautifully restored 300-year-old thatched cottage, or detour to Nagoro – also known as the Scarecrow Village – where life-sized dolls outnumber residents.

(L) Iya no Kazura-bashi vine bridge; (T) The verdant Iya Valley; (B) Bird's eye view of Ōboke Gorge

Kōchi

(T) Sakamoto Ryoma Memorial Museum in Kōchi

Sun-kissed Kōchi sits dead in the centre of Shikoku's southern arc, a palm-lined, river-laced city with shopping arcades and trams that trundle as if they've got nowhere urgent to be. The headline sight is Kōchi-jō, a compact hilltop fortress reached through the Ōte-mon gate, with a three-storey donjon that still feels properly feudal. Come on a Sunday and the city tilts into the huge market on Otesuji-dōri, as farmers roll in from all over the prefecture and the street turns into a long, edible corridor. When hunger turns serious, duck into Hirome Ichiba at the end of the Obiya-machi arcade, where sixty-plus stalls, cheap beer and *katsuo* (bonito tuna) dishes make mingling almost unavoidable. For a breather, ride up to Godai-san-kōen for wide views across the harbour, then step next door into Chikurin-ji, Temple 31 on the 88-temple Shikoku Pilgrimage.

Matsuyama & Dōgo Onsen

Matsuyama is Shikoku's largest city, but it wears its size lightly. Trams give it an old-fashioned grace as they rattle between the hill of Matsuyama-jō and the onsen suburb of Dōgo, 2km east. The castle ride is part of the fun – ropeway or chairlift up Katsuyama, then wide views across the city to the shimmering Seto Inland Sea. After that, Dōgo takes over. Dōgo Onsen Honkan is an 1894 architectural extravaganza, crowned by a heron statue, with baths that range from the lively Kami-no-yu to the more exclusive Tama-no-yu, plus the drained imperial Yūshinden. The souvenir shops and a faintly seedy edge come with the territory, but once you're in a *yukata* (traditional summer kimono) with tea and snacks, you'll forgive a lot. Just off the main drag, duck into Tsubaki-no-yu, a modern bathhouse with a big granite tub fed from the same source, popular with elderly locals who take their bathing seriously.

(O) The castle tower at Matsuyama-jō; (L) Dōgo Onsen clock; (B) Elaborate architecture at Dōgo Onsen

Kyūshū

Kyūshū is Japan's volcanic south, closer to Korea than Tokyo and packed with big scenery. One day you're slurping ramen at riverside stalls in Fukuoka, the next you're hiking the rim of Aso-san's vast caldera or soaking in onsen steam in Beppu. Nagasaki brings a cosmopolitan harbour and complex history, while the island's southern reaches simmer with ash, forests and coastal light. It's a thrilling alternative adventure to the usual circuits.

大ちゃん
博多長浜
ラーメン
串焼
牛タン
おでん
ラーメン

Fukuoka

Fukuoka is Kyūshū's gateway and its most likeable city, with a confident, late-night streak. Tenjin presents the slick downtown core of boutiques, department stores and fashion buildings, but the city's real pull comes after dark, when food stalls pop up and the air fills with steam and chatter. Across the Naka-gawa, Nakasu is an entertainment district on a sandbank that somehow crams in around two thousand restaurants and bars, at its most atmospheric when the riverbanks line with food carts. When you want something odd and modern, Canal City's multicoloured blocks wrap around an indoor "canal" that erupts with jets of water and evening light shows. For a slower pace, Ōhori-kōen's lake and islets sit on the old castle grounds, while Hakata Machiya Furusato-kan offers a glimpse of Hakata's late nineteenth- and early twentieth-century world, plus the craft traditions that shape the city.

(L) Yatai, local food stalls

Nagasaki

Nagasaki is Kyūshū's most cosmopolitan city, built around a magnificent harbour and shaped by outside influence. It was Japan's only link with Europe for two centuries, when Dutch merchants were confined to the tiny artificial island of Dejima, now impressively reconstructed. The city's complex history is most visible in Urakami, where the hypocentre area includes the Peace Park and the gruelling but informative Nagasaki Atomic Bomb Museum. Between the two, trams stitch together backstreets, a tight Chinatown, quiet temple rows and the bars and clubs of Shianbashi. Down south, preserved European houses on the old hilltop concession – today's Glover Garden – look out over the water, and the city still carries Japan's strongest Christian thread. Finish with a twilight ropeway ride up Inasa-yama, timed for when the harbour lights snap on.

(L) Kōshi-byō Confucius Shrine in Nagasaki; (T) At the city's lantern festival; (B) Looking down on Nagasaki from Mount Inasa

Kumamoto-jō

Kumamoto-jō is the kind of castle that makes most others look merely decorative. Completed in 1607 after just seven years' work, it is one of Japan's largest and most impressive castles, a fortress of steep stonework and sly design touches that feel like they were drawn up by someone who expected trouble. Lord Katō Kiyomasa built it as both a war machine and a showpiece, with *musha-gaeshi* walls engineered to defeat climbers, wells sunk for sieges, and camphor and ginkgo planted for the long haul. It was tested for real in 1877, when Saigō Takamori's rebels besieged it for fifty days. The castle held, then burnt. Restored in 1960, it was battered again by the 2016 earthquake, yet the main keep is open and the walk up through the west-flank park still delivers the full, fearsome impact that the castle was designed to have.

(O) Kumamoto's castle; (L) Statue of Katō Kiyomasa in front of Kumamoto-jō; (T) The hall in Honmaru-goten Palace

Aso Caldera

(T) Looking towards Aso Caldera

Aso Caldera is Kyūshū at its most volcanic: a vast bowl of mountains with an active, smouldering core that can turn the landscape otherworldly in minutes. When the alert level allows, you can ride up from Aso Station and walk to the smoking crater of Naka-dake, catching glimpses of a seething grey lake through turbulent, sulphurous clouds of steam. Drop back down for Kusasenri, a grassy bowl speckled with shallow crater lakes, where a ninety-minute circuit takes in the crumpled peak of Eboshi-dake. For a quieter high point, climb Kishimadake, an easy half-hour up grassy slopes with big views over the caldera and across to Naka-dake, then down into its extinct crater. Any visit to Aso rewards flexibility: check conditions before tackling it, take what the volcano gives you, and you'll come away with a day that feels truly elemental.

Beppu & Kannawa

Beppu is less a town than a full-scale hot-spring event, with steam billowing from the drains in the manner of a Manhattan film noir. You feel it before you see it, and once you've clocked the onsen pipes snaking along the streets, resistance to the town's purpose is futile. The classic itinerary is to start old-school at Takegawara, then work your way north to Kannawa for the *jigoku*, where the ground hisses and bubbles and the air smells sulphurous. Slot in a sand bath when you need a reset, then take the ropeway up Tsurumi-dake for views across the bay – Shikoku can be seen on a clear day. Finish in the forests above town, tracking down the hidden onsen that make Beppu feel strangely magical despite all the plumbing. The town also eats well. Look out for *jigoku mushi* – vegetables and eggs slow-cooked in steam from the "hells" – a Kannawa snack that tastes better than it sounds.

(O) Steam rises from the Beppu bathhouses;
(L) A jigoku demon statue stands guard; (T) Red-coloured onsen waters; (B) Shrine at Umi Jigoku hot spring

お会計
CASHIER

Yufuin

Yufuin comes as a breather after Beppu's full-throttle onsen spectacle. The most satisfying way in is the slow, scenic route over the mountains, arriving with that small shift in air and tempo that tells you you're out of the city. It also connects neatly with Beppu by bus, which makes it an easy combination if you want to experience both *jigoku* theatrics and something calmer. Treat Yufuin as an onsen stop designed for strolling between baths and meals rather than chasing "sights", then move on when you feel reset. Yufuin is also ideal if you want your hot springs with a side of fresh air. The shape of Yufu-dake dominates the skyline, and the town makes a good base for getting out into the surrounding hills before returning for a long soak and an early night.

(L) Yufuin's picturesque village; (T) Looking out over the shrine of Tenso-jinja; (B) Lake Kinrin-ko, at the base of Yufu-dake

Takachiho Gorge & shrine country

Takachiho sits on the Kumamoto–Miyazaki border, where the Gokase-gawa has sliced a narrow channel through ancient lava and left a landscape that looks engineered by myth. The gorge is the headline. At its tightest it's just 3m wide, dropping 100m between basalt columns that fan out like a giant cockleshell. Get down to Mihashi Bridge, rent a rowing boat, and the emerald-green river turns the whole thing theatrical, especially beneath Manai Waterfall. Back in town, Takachiho-jinja is a simple wooden shrine engulfed in ancient cryptomeria, with nightly Yokagura dances that pull local legend into the present. Then push east to Amano Iwato-jinja, set among venerable cedars, and walk on to Amano Yasugawara, the cave where the gods supposedly gathered when Amaterasu hid the world in darkness – a hush of candles, stones and cedar shade after the glare of the gorge.

(O) Rowing up to waterfalls at Takachiho Gorge; (L) Snaking roads up to the gorge; (T) Takachiho-jinja has an atmospheric setting

Kirishima National Park

Sprawling across the Kagoshima–Miyazaki border, Kirishima National Park is a compact riot of volcanic geography that has earned it the nickname Volcano Museum. More than twenty volcanic mountains rise and fall around ten crater lakes, with hot springs seeping out wherever the rock gives up. The traditional approach is via Kirishima-jingū, a truly delightful shrine shrouded by cryptomeria trees, with bright vermilion torii and a red-lacquer bridge setting the tone. From here you can work towards Takachiho-no-mine, the peak tied to the legend of Ninigi-no-mikoto's descent. For the best walking, head up to Ebino Kōgen. The centre is a bleak car park and a clutch of cafés, but step behind the visitor centre and a 4km trail threads through red pine and maple to three perfectly round, cobalt-blue crater lakes, with a free hot-spring footbath waiting at the end.

(L) Hiking in Kirishima National Park

Kagoshima & Sakurajima

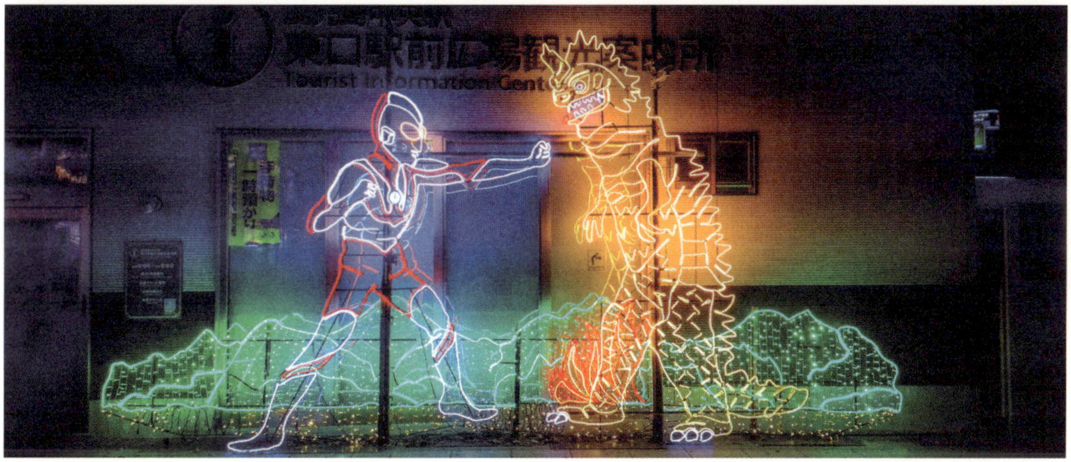

Kagoshima has a breezy, southern edge, but the city's real drama sits right there in the bay. Climb Shiroyama through stands of mature subtropical trees and the view opens out over Kagoshima and the smouldering cone of Sakurajima, just 4km away. Down below, the Satsuma story of samurai power and modernization is close to the surface, from Terukuni-jinja tucked into Shiroyama's greenery to the bullet-pocked remnants and carp-filled moats of Tsurumaru-jō, with Saigō Takamori looming in bronze nearby. Then swap history for geology. The ferry runs round the clock and takes fifteen minutes, long enough for a quick stop at a noodle-bar. On Sakurajima, take the road up to Yunohira Observatory for the closest legal look at the deeply creviced summit, then circle past 1914 lava fields and the *torii* of Kurokami-jinja, half-buried in ash and pumice.

(L) Sakurajima looming behind Kagoshima's cityscape; (T) Downtown Kagoshima; (B) Neon figures downtown

Yakushima

(T) Intense green hues in Yakushima's rainforest

Yakushima is all craggy peaks and wave after wave of dripping rainforest, rising steeply from the sea some 60km off Cape Sata. It rains hard and often, which is why the island's vegetation shifts so dramatically, from subtropical coast to subarctic peaks. Most people come for the cedars. In Shiratani Unsuikyō, dank, mossy and mysterious, easy loops take you past waterfalls and ancient Yaku-sugi in old-growth laurel forest. Go bigger and you're into Jōmon-sugi territory, a five-hour hike to a mossy, tattered trunk 16.4m around that looks more like rock face than living tissue, with Wilson's Stump as a surreal waypoint. When your legs give up, head south to Onoaida for a seaside onsen at Hirauchi Kaichū, a hot rock pool that only appears around low tide, or snorkel at Isso and Nakama.

昭和四十三

Okinawa

Mention Okinawa to mainland Japanese and you'll often get a wistful sigh. Warm weather, clear seas rich with marine life, unspoiled beaches, lush jungles and a notably laid-back atmosphere combine to make it Japan's favourite escape. The Ryūkyū Shotō – more than a hundred subtropical islands – stretch 700km from Kyūshū to Yonaguni-jima, within sight of Taiwan on a clear day. Coral reefs, top-class dive sites and winter sun await the weary traveller.

Naha & Shuri

Naha should, in theory, be a place to sort out ferries and flights before moving on, yet it's oddly easy to get stuck here – in a good way. Kokusai-dōri draws the crowds with its souvenir sprawl, but the real texture lies just south in the covered arcades of the Makishi Public Market area, where stalls pile up tropical fruit, every conceivable cut of pork and ice-packed arrays of reef fish. For craft and colour, detour into Tsuboya, the pottery district founded in 1682, still dotted with workshops and galleries – and keep an eye out for snarling *shisa* guardians. Shuri lifts the story onto higher ground. Shuri-jō, the royal seat of the Ryūkyū kings, was painstakingly restored in the early 1990s, then badly damaged by fire in 2019, with restoration due to be fully complete in late 2026. Combine it with the excellent Okinawa Prefectural Museum on the route back towards town.

(L) Taking part in an ancient new year ceremony at Shuri-jō

Yanbaru

Yanbaru National Park is Okinawa-Hontō's northern green heart, where the island stops feeling suburban and starts feeling truly wild. Villages sit among dense forest, and the old way of life still survives in pockets, a quieter counterpoint to the built-up south. This is where Okinawa's reputation for biodiversity comes into focus. Beyond the reefs offshore, the forests are home to endemic species, including Pryer's woodpecker and the crested serpent eagle, along with plenty of less glamorous life in the undergrowth. It also has the habu, a dark green, highly venomous snake that likes dense vegetation and roadsides more than people, so watch where you step and keep your hands out of leafy holes. Come for rainforest walks and the distinctively humid, bird-filled atmosphere, then cool off with a swim on the way back down the coast.

(L) A T-rex at DINO Dinosaur Park Yanbaru Subtropical Forest; (T) The cliff face of Cape Hedo, Yanbaru National Park; (B) Remote waterfalls and pools in the forest

Kerama Islands

The Kerama Islands sit just 30km offshore from Naha, a knot of 22 islands and sand-and-coral fragments scattered across a startlingly clear sea. Only four are inhabited, which helps explain their appeal. Beaches here are among Okinawa's most unspoiled, the offshore reefs offer superb diving, and since 2014 much of the archipelago has been a national park. Base yourself on sleepy Zamami-jima, where a whale statue greets the ferries and winter brings a boom in humpback whale watching, with boats heading out from late January to April. When the whales move on, the water stays warm enough for swimming and snorkelling well into December. Furuzamami has excellent coral and shoals of multicoloured fish, while calmer Ama beach can reward visitors with sightings of sea turtles when the tide is right. Bring a mask, take it slow, and let the islands speak for themselves.

(O) Idyllic coastline; (L) Eastern pale clouded yellow butterfly; (T) Diving with a Hawksbill turtle

Miyako-jima

(T) Rocks scatter the shoreline at Miyako-jima

Miyako-jima is flat, triangular and oddly enticing. Roads run through field after field of sugar cane, with the island's main town, Hirara, sitting on the northwest coast as a practical base for eating, drinking and beach-hopping. The "sights" are mostly the coastline. Sunayama Beach, reached via a steep, winding path and a sand dune, has that first-glimpse wow factor, and sunset can line up neatly with a natural stone arch. At the eastern tip, Higashi Henna-zaki is a 2km-long peninsula of wild flowers and wide views, with excellent snorkelling beaches just to the north at Yoshino and Aragusuku. If you want even more space, cross the bridge to Ikema-jima for quieter sands and coral, or take a glass-bottomed boat out to Yaebishi Reef when low spring tides expose it. When you tire of perfection, Hirara's Traditional Arts and Crafts Centre brings you back to a quieter world of handwork and tradition with delicate Miyako-jōfu weaving.

Yaeyama Islands

The Yaeyama Islands feel like Okinawa turned up a notch: further south, slower, and closer to Taiwan in spirit as well as geography. Ishigaki-jima is the hub, a mountainous island with enough facilities to make it a practical base, plus quick ferries that tempt you into easy island-hopping. Taketomi-jima is the palate cleanser, tiny, beach-fringed, almost no traffic, with a languid, end-of-the-line feel that suits a late afternoon and an unhurried night. Iriomote-jima is the wild card. Often described as Japan's last wilderness, it trades in rainforest, mangroves, kayaking and trekking, with the added frisson of unique wildlife, including the elusive Iriomote cat. Most people come for the scenery and watersports, but Yaeyama's real hook is the way the islands keep pulling you further out, one ferry ride at a time.

(L) The northernmost point of Ishigaki-jima; (T) Ishigaki's lagoon; (B) Atmospheric Iriomote

Publishing information

Japan • 100 Legendary Places
Editor: Sarah Clark
Proofreader: Beth Williams
Designer: Michał Ptasznik
Picture Editor: Piotr Kala
Picture Manager: Tom Smyth
Production Operations Manager: Katie Bennett
Publishing Technology Manager: Rebeka Davies
Head of Publishing: Sarah Clark

Our selection
Japan • 100 Legendary Places offers our curation of the most exceptional destinations in the country, with choices and content based on *Rough Guides Japan*. Recent contributors to *Rough Guides Japan* include Martin Zatko and Rebecca Hallet.

First Edition 2026

ISBN: 9781835296455

Printed by Finidr in Czech Republic

A catalogue record for this book is available from the British Library.

MIX
Paper | Supporting responsible forestry
FSC® C014138
FSC www.fsc.org

Distribution
UK, Ireland and Europe
Apa Publications (UK) Ltd; mail@roughguides.com
United States and Canada
Two Rivers; ips@ ingramcontent.com
Australia and New Zealand
Woodslane; info@woodslane.com.au
Worldwide
Apa Publications (UK) Ltd; mail@roughguides.com

Special Sales, Content Licensing and CoPublishing
Rough Guides can be purchased in bulk quantities at discounted prices. We can create special editions, personalized jackets and corporate imprints tailored to your needs.
mail@roughguides.com; http://roughguides.com

EU Representative
LOGOS EUROPE, 9 rue Nicolas Poussin, 17000, LA ROCHELLE, France
Contact@logoseurope.eu; +33 (0) 667937378

Photo credits

All images Shutterstock except:
Alamy 62/63, 113T, 118/119, 175T, 213R, 235T
Aomori Prefecture 44/45

Cover credit: Mount Fuji at sunset, from Chureito Pagoda **Shutterstock**

Caption key
(L) = left
(R) = right
(T) = top
(B) = bottom
(O) = opposite

Japan *is* waiting

Make the **legend** your own

中央区
銀座七丁目
Ginza 7
観光
岩崎ビル
Brillia
MITSUKOSHI
8-20